GW00418629

The Running Year

THE RUNNING YEAR

Sebastian and Peter Coe

To Junder
Best wishes
Sebastian Coe

A FITNESS LOG AND DIARY
1987

PAVILION
MICHAEL JOSEPH

First published in great Britain in 1986
by Pavilion Books Limited
196 Shaftesbury Avenue, London WC2H 8JL
in association with Michael Joseph Limited
44 Bedford Square, London WC1B 3DP

Copyright © 1986 Sebastian Coe

All rights reserved. No part of the publication may
be reproduced, stored in a retrieval system, or
transmitted, in any form or by any means, electronic,
mechanical, photocopying, recording or otherwise,
without the prior permission of the copyright holders.

Designed by Lawrence Edwards

Editorial Consultant: Nick Mason

British Library Cataloguing in Publication Data

Coe, Sebastian
  The running year : a fitness diary and log.
  1. Running
  I. Title II. Coe, Peter, *1919*–
  796.4'26   GV1061

  ISBN 0–907516–80–7

The photographs in this diary are reproduced by kind
permission of the following:

Mark Shearman: 18, 50, 62, 98, 99, 135, 136, 141, 148,
150, 152, 185; *The Times:* Chris Cole 6; Ian Stewart 7;
Steve Bent 52; Suresh Karadia 58–59, 105;
Sunday Times: Tom Stoddart (inset) 105, 107;
Hugh Hastings: 14, 16, 55, 142, 144, 146, 147;
Allsport: 20; Trevor Jones 60; Tony Duffy 65, 101;
David Cannon 192; Colorsport: 56, 96;
Sporting Pictures (UK) Ltd: 2, 94;
Associated Sports: George Herringshaw 103;
Peter Coe: 12

Drawings by Emma Coe

Printed and bound in Great Britain by
Butler & Tanner Ltd, Frome, Somerset

Contents

Foreword

Sebastian Coe

I have been keeping a training diary regularly for the last fifteen years, and over the last ten, since I have been running as a serious competitor, the entries have been full and detailed.

My diary is indispensable, for two reasons. First, it gives me instant recall over my current training period: I can see how much work I have done over the past few weeks, how much I should have done, how much I'm improving, how minor adjustments might be made to my workload. Secondly, it allows me to look back over the years; one athletics season tends to resemble any other in terms of important dates and major meetings, so a diary can help me re-create the build-up patterns of times and effort and workload that succeeded in the past, or perhaps help modify those that didn't work quite as well as they should have done.

Whatever your level of running, it must be worthwhile quantifying what you do in training. If it's important for me to have these facts written down methodically, so it is for a runner with two or three years of fun-running behind him who wants to run a marathon. The diary will be a genuine aid to training, a perfect guide book if he ever trains for a long race again, and, if his comments on his own progress are frank enough, an amusing piece of nostalgic reading for winter evenings in years to come.

Over the months you will probably devise a shorthand of your own, as I have, to pack even more useful information into the log; but however much it contains I am sure it will prove an invaluable part of your running life.

Good luck!

Introduction

Peter Coe

For success in any endeavour you need a plan, and to ensure good results the plan has to be monitored. The course of training is never perfectly smooth for fun-runner or for superstar, and while it is wise to have an overall training plan it does not mean that any runner, whatever his or her aims or abilities, should have an inflexible 365-day programme to be enforced regardless of circumstances.

We do catch colds in winter, we do miss a step on the stairs and sprain an ankle and we do get jobs or study assignments or family commitments that take us away for various periods. These diversions are not causes for great concern. No one is obliged to turn out for a late run on a bitter night just to accommodate a late session in the office or overtime on the factory floor.

Provided that in any training period—say two weeks, or even a month—you have near enough completed the planned work, there is little to worry about. Just as long as the harder sessions are followed by those allowing adequate recovery ('one hard then two easy', or whatever your physical status requires) then all will be well.

But how best to keep track of your progress, and to restore the balance of sessions to meet your overall plan?

That is where this Runner's Diary will prove invaluable. It offers not only instant recall of what you have done, but also when it was done, how hard it was and in what sequence you did it. For the novice and the star alike this is reassurance. For the star, and equally importantly the star's coach, it is also a ready reference to those pre-race build-ups and count-downs that preceded exceptional performances. Conversely, it can provide the clues as to why a performance was poor, or why you are feeling below par or just plain sluggish.

A proper training diary is at the very least a record of progress and a useful aid to fitness. For many runners it is an absolute must—we still refer to Seb's diaries as far back as 1973 and 1974, and find in them new food for thought.

In his excellent book, *A Scientific Approach to Distance Running*, Dr David Costill makes this very important observation: 'Although measurements of muscle glycogen and blood haemoglobin concentrations may sound the alarm of over-training, the runner's sensations of effort and the stop-watch are more reliable indices of staleness. The best way to determine a runner's required ratio of training to rest is to keep a training diary of mileage/intensity, performance and *subjective observations.*' (My italics)

It's what you, the runner, think and feel, over the weeks and months of training, that is the best indication of progress. And the only way to record that is to write it down.

Logging your progress

Every piece of information relevant to your running can be useful, and most of what you will want to enter in the day-to-day log will be self-evident. One or two sections, though, might seem unusual:

Sleep   How many hours did you have the previous night (and were they restful or not)? Any changes in pattern might be reflected in a change in your performances.

Heart rate   This is a record of your *resting* heart rate (best observed on waking each day). New runners can expect to see their heart rate come down,but consistency is what you are after, and only if it goes *up* is there any cause for concern.

Weight   If you are fit, don't expect your weight to go down just because you are running regularly—you will probably be eating more to compensate for the energy loss. If you are worried about variations in your weight, you may need to adjust your diet.

Perceived effort   This is a subjective assessment of how hard you have been working. It attempts neither to assess the amount of work done, nor the rate at which it is done—only how hard you have found it.

An improvement in the time taken for a run is not the only way to measure progress. A reduction in the mental and physical effort required is also a good guide, sometimes the best one.

Training is the correct application of increasing doses of stress over a carefully assessed range, each dose being followed by an adequate period of recovery. It would be destructive indeed if every time a runner performed over any distance he sought to reduce the time taken for it. This would not be building up, and it would result in breaking down.

Each improvement in time takes every runner on to a new level of fitness. He should then consolidate this new achievement so that it becomes repeatable. The next decision is when to attempt the next level of fitness, and a simple indicator is when the effort required to perform the current task has come down to, say, 85 or 90 per cent of the initial effort.

This assessment will be a subjective one, and it is only with practice that the runner will consistently be able to gauge the level of his feelings. Remember, it is *perceived* effort; that means it will vary according to a number of factors, not only the runner's general feeling of well-being or tiredness on the day concerned, but also on the wind, the temperature and the conditions underfoot. With experience a runner will be able to make allowances in his mind for all this, and in time cross-country runs in daylight, evening road runs in winter and summer repetitions on the track will become equally easy to assess.

An aid to consistency in assessment is a numbered descriptive chart, starting at 1 on the scale ('very easy') and increasing in steps to 20 ('extremely severe', 'exhausting'). It might seem obvious that the more steps there are—the more gradual the change from one degree of effort to another—the more accurate and helpful it will be to assessment. However, having to think too much or ponder too long will tend to spoil the accuracy of the assessment. The following table should be quite detailed enough:

1	Very easy	(Borg, 1971)
2		
3		
4		
5	Easy	
6		
7		
8		
9		
10	Moderate	
11		
12		
13		
14		
15	Hard	
16		
17		
18		
19		
20	Extremely severe	

Your assessment is likely to be more realistic if you make it immediately after the run or the task is completed. The way you feel after training sessions is a good indication of how well you are coping with your total stress—your lifestyle and your training load.

Looking back

Old training diaries are mines of instant nostalgia. The longer you keep them, the more irresistible they become, and a glance through a page or two of scrawled handwriting and scribbled figures from half a lifetime ago can bring back vivid memories of those training days when my running career had barely begun.

I'm looking, as I write, at the diary Peter and I kept for the 1973 season. I was sixteen then, and the plan was to have a go at the national championships just to see how good I really was.

I remember now that I was very ambitious even then, and totally committed to winning. I had finished a good cross-country season with the school and with Hallamshire Harriers, so the base of steady distance work was there on which to build in the summer.

I was lucky that year: the English Schools championships were a good month before the AAA Youth Championships, so I would be able to test myself out at 3,000 metres in the earlier competition, have a rest, and then go for the 1500 metres at the Youth Championships, which was my real target for the summer.

Running my eye down the training schedules for the fortnight before those two events takes me right back to the roads and hills and fields of Yorkshire and Derbyshire and the local track at Sheffield. After Day 1 of the build-up, taken up with short speed repetitions, there I am on Day 2 in good old Graves Park, with its wonderful three-mile circuit of woods, hills and rolling grass—just the place for a hard six-mile cross-country work-out. (I remember it equally well, though with somewhat less pleasure, in the winter, when the wind-chill factor high above the city of Sheffield, snow or no snow, left you feeling that there was nothing between you and the Urals.)

Day 3 takes me back to the undulating valley road on the edge of Sheffield and its half-mile repetitions with short recoveries—tremendous for developing speed endurance, terrible for appreciating the beauties of the Rivelin Valley. Day 7 brings me back to the rolling hills of Graves Park, and Day 10, in another flood of nostalgia, to our very own front door.

Day 10 was hill training, and unforgettable. When we left our front door to run, any direction was up. And Roslin Road was more up than most—100 metres of uneven pavement straight up a one-in-six hill. First, then, a couple of miles up Manchester Road for a good warm-up, then the attack on Roslin. Thirty fast runs up the hill, thirty jogs down it for what was supposed to be a recovery. I can remember even now having to force myself to complete the session with another two-mile run to warm down, made all the more agonising by the fact that our house was just round the corner.

It all paid off, as the diary reminds me, and the win in the Schools 3,000 metres was easier than we had dared to hope. And that breathing space before the next big build-up, with some of the pressure off, feels good and relaxed even from thirteen years' distance.

A couple of weeks on, though, and the diary is recording the major build-up of the season—the AAA Youth 1500 metres. Every week that summer contained, as has every summer since, one long run. That period saw it increase from six to nine miles, and Day 2 saw me on the moors at Moscar Top, crossing the hills and valleys and taking the steep descent into Low Bradfield and back towards Sheffield through some of the most wonderful scenery in England. (Memories of those runs tell me that it was always summertime; the subconscious has done its best to erase the winter mornings on those moors, fighting my way through drifting snow from Yorkshire Bridge up to Ringinglow.)

By Day 8 the long run was no longer but rather harder, testing me once again on the grassy slopes of Graves Park. Then a rest day. Then the real sharpening-up, which began on Day 10: 7 × 800 metres, the key to my best form then, as it is even now. These were a series of road runs, nearly flat out, pursued in those days by the old man keeping the headlights of the family car uncomfortably close to my rear end. He was kinder in those days: he let me have three minutes recovery after each 800 metres; but even that seemed to last no longer than the time it took him to shout the time of the last run, turn on the engine and start the torture again.

Day 14, says the diary, saw the training end with the 1500 metres heats. And Day 15 saw everything turn out right, with me front-running in lane two all the way, determined not to get boxed in, and pulling away to win my first UK title in a championship best time.

Training in 1973 wasn't all hard pre-race build-up, and the eye tends to skate over the frequent, draining, repetitive but invaluable sessions on that Sheffield track. But there is no better confidence-builder than a minute or two with the old diaries and their welcome reminder that 'If I could do that as a lad, I can do it as a man.'   **SC**

First steps

Running is natural, whether you are five years old or fifty. Most people beginning a conscious fitness programme, though, will not have run in earnest for some time (running to the bus stop with briefcase or shopping basket doesn't count). Generally, two things are likely to cause you concern: Will it do me any harm? And what is the best way to begin?

Health

If you feel well, the chances are that you *are* well. In practice, the only serious risks in running are connected with heart problems, and since stress ECG and other laboratory tests are not readily available to most people, the following simple check list should help allay any worries.

Family history Is there any record of heart trouble?
Personality Are you highly strung? Do you have a tendency to be hyped up, or to operate under great stress?
Obesity Are you seriously overweight?
Tobacco Do you smoke a lot? All smoking is inadvisable, and heavy smoking increases the risk of death from a heart attack.
Effort Do you feel distressed by increased effort of a normal kind: stairs, gardening, hurrying for a bus?

If your answer to any of the above is Yes, it would be as well to seek medical advice before you start running. If your doctor is sympathetic to running, or to exercise in general, so much the better.

Walk before you run

This is a safe-for-all start-up programme, suitable for any age or occupation, man or woman.
1. Let at least two hours elapse from the last meal.
2. Wear the shoes and clothes you intend to run in.
3. Walking as briskly as you can, see if you can cover a measured mile without great discomfort. Deep breathing is all right, panting and wheezing is not. Learn to walk the mile in about fifteen minutes. You are also learning to sustain a heart rate of about 140/150 per minute.

4. Re-start the walking when the heart rate falls to about 120 per minute—this recovery should not take more than five to six minutes.

5. Extend this training until you can walk for thirty minutes maintaining the 140/150 heart rate.

6. Your target should now be steady walking for one hour, during which you should manage to cover four miles. By now you will find that your heart rate on waking will be perceptibly slower.

7. Now start jogging. Do this by walking quicker and quicker until it feels easier to jog rather than walk. There are dozens of different opinions as to what exactly distinguishes jogging from running, and a jog to an athlete would certainly constitute a punishing work-out to a lesser mortal; but in general, depending on age and fitness, a time definition of jogging could be something between a 10-minute-mile and a 12-minute-mile pace.

Continue jogging until the fatigue is moderately uncomfortable, then drop back into a walk. Start jogging again as soon as you can, and continue for as long as you can without distress. As before, deep breathing is all right, panting or gasping for breath is not. Repeat daily until you can jog for one hour.

8. Now you can start jogging and running, just as you did with walking and jogging, until you can run for an hour.

Well done. You are now a runner. **PC**

Cold comfort

It was a grey, uninviting winter morning in Chicago, and they told me that outside it was 38 degrees below freezing. I don't think I can have ever worn so much clothing in my life at any time, let alone when starting out on a run. I was wearing three or four layers of clothing, top and bottom, and two pairs of gloves; in that sort of cold you have to have a scarf across your mouth because it's dangerous breathing in a lot of air when it's so cold; you have to wear at least one hat; most people wear glasses or goggles to prevent their eyes freezing up—just about the only patches of bare skin open to the elements were two spots round my cheekbones.

Of course, it's quite impossible to do anything of value—all I got out of it was a strange sort of spartan satisfaction at having actually completed a distance run in such conditions . . . and, I suppose, the reassurance that nothing I was ever going to have to face up to in England would be as absurdly cold as that.

Runners in Britain have become a pretty hardy breed. Anyone who trains seriously around the calendar in this country is going to have to run in all sorts of weather, and on balance the conditions are going to be more or less miserable for quite a portion of the year. I'm lucky enough to be able to get away to somewhere warmer if the winter drags on and really gets in the way of the early season training, but even that would only be for a week or so—for the rest of the winter we're all at the mercy of the weather.

My own attitude is full of contradictions. I make no secret of the fact that I really do not like running in the cold; it may be something to do with my style, which is so dependent on my being able to maintain a fluidity of movement, and which just grinds into slow motion when I really get cold. On the other hand, I positively dislike running with a lot of clothing on. It's very rare for me to run in gloves—my hands almost always warm up naturally after a couple of miles, and then they keep their warmth for as long as I keep moving. I can usually manage with a pair of long trousers or tracksuit bottoms, and an extra layer on top—probably a rain-top to keep out the wind. These tops are far better ventilated nowadays; you can have a good run in one of them without ending up as a wet, soggy mess of sweat, which is what the old rain-suits used to specialise in.

Underfoot, too, the cold has its contradictions. It really is *not* possible to run on ice—on pavements or paths—without running a real risk of injury. Even if you do survive you have no chance of maintaining any sort of style, and you are calling into play all sorts of extra, untrained muscle groups just to prevent yourself falling over. On the other hand, there's nothing so enjoyable, once in a while, as running over virgin

snow; it's hard work, a bit like running through soft sand, and I wouldn't want to do it every day, but the exhilaration can add a much needed ration of pleasure to training in winter.

Generally, though, I put up with cold weather rather than revel in it; and I hate having to compete in the cold. That goes for the summer months as well: it's a familiar complaint that there are so few record attempts made on the track in Britain, let alone record-breaking achievements, but the reason is simple. A cool evening at Crystal Palace, when the light fades and the breeze starts to quicken, can tighten up the muscles as surely as the winter wind on a Yorkshire hillside. It only needs a drop of two or three degrees in the air temperature, and suddenly a proportion of your effort is being spent keeping the body warm and supple.

It's all relative, though. The drop in temperature after a hot day in Italy, or even in summer in Scandinavia, can produce a cool, still calmness that we hardly ever experience in Britain — ideal for spectators and perfect for athletes. Those are the kind of evenings we can dream about when we're out in the early morning freezing fog in February. They're well worth waiting for. **SC**

Dressing the part

You won't run any better if you go out dressed like a fashion plate; you *will* run better if all the gear you have selected does its job efficiently and without causing discomfort. The rule is simple; buy only what you need, and make sure that if fulfils the purpose for which it was bought. Function is the guide, not fashion.

In Britain we run in any number of sets of weather conditions, from the cold, wet and wind of winter to the hot sun of midsummer. A good running wardrobe will cater for any variation in temperature or weather.

Winter clothing should be light if at all possible, but it should also be completely windproof, and above all it should 'breathe'. A rain suit—the top layer whenever rain or snow is expected—should be light and, of course, waterproof, but it should also be well ventilated. No training suit should be allowed to get soggy with perspiration (some of the new synthetic fibres, with their syphoning effect, perform this function admirably).

A rain-suit hood that folds neatly into its own back is preferable to one that hangs loosely, generally flapping about and often collecting water. These suits should have long zips over the legs so that you can take them off and on without removing your shoes. If you are training on roads in the dark, a light-coloured top, or an orange or green reflective strip on tracksuit top or trousers, is a good idea.

The choice of headgear is very personal. Seb rarely wears any, regardless of the weather, but some people find a head-covering absolutely necessary. The old woollen balaclava will probably itch over a long run but a woolly hat can be pulled down over the ears in the most extreme cold.

In general, a gradually acquired hardiness is the best defence against the rigours of midwinter running, but the odd pair of light cotton gloves may offer a lot of comfort.

Summer clothing should, of course, be light, and should allow air to circulate freely. Heat-reflecting colours (white or light pastel shades) keep you cooler than dark colours, and in very hot conditions a light ventilated peaked cap might help, both by reflecting light and heat away from the head, and by shading the face; but again ventilation is crucial, and the hat should be open at the back, or have mesh vents sewn in.

Fit for the job Both in summer and in winter, remember that comfort is the principal aim. Vests or singlets should not be so snug a fit that they stop air circulating, nor so loose that they slip awkwardly off the shoulder. Shorts and training trousers should allow maximum freedom, but they should neither be baggy nor a case of elasticated strangulation (indeed, elastic exerts continuous pressure and is always restricting; the old draw-strings do not). All seams should be neat, particularly where they come into contact with the skin, so that they do not chafe or irritate. It is worth experimenting to find which of the dozens of sock designs on the market suits you best, but you will certainly need an absorbent, cushion-soled model for distance work and general training; socks need to fit as perfectly as shoes, otherwise soreness or blisters will be a danger.

Three of each So long as you can afford the outlay, 'three of each' is a good rule — one in use, one in the wash, one spare. A basic wardrobe might consist of: three singlets; three pairs of running shorts (and, for men, underpants or abdominal supports if they are not built into the shorts); three pairs of absorbent, cushion-soled socks; two tracksuits and one rain-suit; three long-sleeved running vests/shirts; three sweat shirts. Most women will need running bras as well. You should be able to get by with two pairs of training shoes, but be careful not to wear them out at the same time, or you'll be left without a spare pair. (Serious competitive runners will, of course, have specialist shoes for their own events — road, track, cross-country — some aspects of which we discuss in more detail on page 63.)

Peripheral articles — headgear, sweatbands and the like — are best borrowed for trial before you buy them. Indeed, it is always best to try out any new kind of clothing before you lay out the money. But if you are stuck with something you are unhappy with, be prepared to change it at once. This may sound expensive advice, but only trial and error can ensure maximum comfort and satisfaction.

Finally, remember that simple and clean gear will serve you well, and will always look right. **PC**

Getting hurt and getting better

One of the immutable certainties of a runner's career is that at one stage or another he is going to be injured. It may not be serious or lasting; it may be the sort of niggling muscle strain that would not make the slightest difference to the day-to-day life of a non-runner. But for someone who runs regularly, it is going to mean frustration, anxiety and, above all, inaction.

Whatever the weather, however great the temptation to stay in a warm house on a wet and windy morning, it literally *is* more difficult for an athlete to stay at home than it is to go out and train. Someone will say, 'You don't want to go out on a day like this,' and you'll probably look out at the clouds and the umbrellas and tacitly agree with them. But within an hour the conscience will begin to nag, and by the end of the morning the guilt of actually having stayed indoors instead of training will be enough to drive you out of your chair, into your running shoes and out on to the street. When injury comes, though, you don't even have the luxury of giving in to the guilt; if your injury is going to get better, you are going to have to remain inactive, and the longer you remain inactive the more frustrating it becomes.

Most runners can recognise the normal niggles and aches, and know from experience how long they are going to take to right themselves; in these cases the frustration is eased by knowing that in a couple of days everything will be back to normal. Anything more serious is a disaster, not least because of the uncertainty of how long it is going to last. My own worst time was in 1983 at the time of the first World Championships. It was illness rather than injury that had put me on the sidelines, but that did nothing to lessen the frustration as the games reached their peak. I was doing anything, even arranging to go away on holiday, to avoid being reminded of what I was missing as the 800 metres and the 1500 metres went ahead without me. I went abroad to get away from the constant television coverage – I would just flick into the local TV station to find out what had been going on, if and when I felt I could take it.

After the frustration comes the anxiety – have you really got over that muscle tear? Is your body really free of the effects of the virus? The first steps back after you get the clearance are tremendously exciting, like starting out on another challenge, but you know you have got weeks of build-up in front of you – you're starting out from a plateau far lower than you have been at for ages.

In my long build-up to the Los Angeles Olympics, after two years interrupted constantly by illness and injury, the questions kept coming back to me, day after day: Is my finishing kick still there? Has my endurance gone? Am I mentally as sharp as I used to be? The trouble was intensified by knowing that these same doubts would be in the minds of the selectors, too.

Questions like this can only be answered by racing, and races at this stage of the build-up are all very jittery and inconclusive. Until you've got a few useful victories— and perhaps a few difficult defeats—under your belt, you can't do more than hint at the answers, even though Olympic finals are only a few weeks away.

There was no way of *proving*, even to myself, that I could run, say, a heat, a semi-final and a final of the 1500 metres in the course of three days and in the same week as four rounds of the 800 metres. The doubts were there up to the moment I was selected, and even then I found myself approaching two heats and the semi-final of the 800 metres, the first really serious competitive races since my lay-off, not absolutely certain that my body was going to be able to stand up to what I was going to demand of it.

In the end things turned out satisfactorily. But it only emphasises how important it is for a runner to have good medical advice close at hand (a doctor sympathetic to sporting activity, a physiotherapist, and a good osteopath, too, in my opinion), and to do everything within reason to avoid injury and illness. It's worth it, just to escape the frustration and the worry.   **SC**

Staying loose

Flexibility can be described as the degree of movement of a part of a body around a joint. People seldom move their body and limbs through their full range of movement, and as a result they acquire a reduced mobility too early in their lives. The problem is accelerated by moving limbs repeatedly through a limited range, and this is exactly what most running demands. Hence the need for exercises which are both corrective and preventive. If the range of movement can be increased, the chances of coming unscathed through an accident,when a limb or a joint might have been over-extended or twisted, are much higher.

When repeated movements are made against a load, the muscles become thicker and stronger, and as a result they tend to become harder and shorter. This puts an added tension on to tendons and increases the risk of injury. Careful static stretching exercises are required to overcome this risk. Of course, stretch requires movement, but to obtain the best effect this movement should be done slowly, and when the point of maximum stretch is reached the position should be held for ten to fifteen seconds.

Sudden and jerky movements, even when exercising, can invoke what is called the myotatic reflex. This is a reaction that activates an opposing muscle or muscles to protect the joint from being damaged. This natural reaction, if it is too fierce or if the muscle is too stiff or cold, can itself tear the muscle, which is precisely what you set out to prevent.

There are specific exercises for specific movements, but the suppling exercises of a hurdler will meet the needs of all runners. Suppling and stretching does not have to be confined to special sessions, and it is wise to do some of these exercises whenever you feel the need—when you have been sitting at a desk for an hour and a half, for example, or standing in the same position for a long time. Get up from your desk now and then, or move from wherever you have been standing, and do some simple bending and stretching. It soon becomes a good habit. And remember the most important rule of stretching: never do it if you are cold, and always start gently.

As you get faster and stronger, you become more susceptible to muscle and tendon injury unless your running progress is matched by a sensible suppling, stretching and strengthening programme. These few exercises will always stand you in good stead, and combined with those we discuss on page 137 they should assure you maximum protection.

There is no satisfaction in filling in the words 'pulled muscle—did not run' in your diary for day after day of convalescence. **PC**

Hamstring stretching I

Hold your ankles with both hands, lower your head to your knees. Hold for 10–15 seconds. Repeat four times.

Hamstring stretching II

Place your ankle on a chair-back, grasp the ankle with both hands and lower your head towards the knee. Repeat two or three times with alternate legs. It's the going down that's difficult — the lower the chair-back, the harder the exercise.

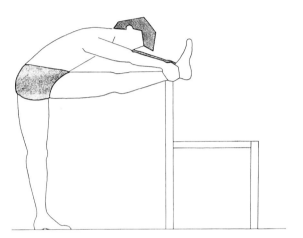

Abdomen stretching and lower back flexibility

This is difficult. Lie on your stomach, and bend your knees back until you can grasp both ankles. Then pull with your legs until your chest is as far off the floor as possible. Hold for 10–15 seconds. Repeat three or four times.

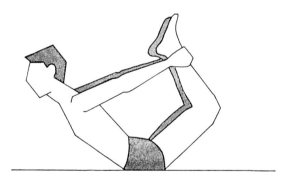

Back flexibility

The 'sagging press-up'. The object is to arch the back as much as possible by straightening your arms and keeping your knees on the ground. The better you get, the closer your pelvis will be to the ground.

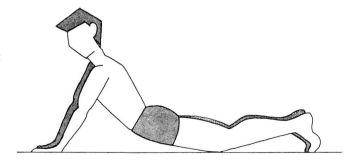

Hip flexibility
Lie flat, pull each knee alternately
as close to your chest as you can.
Move slowly — your body will tell
you when you have stretched it
far enough.

Lower leg muscles
Stand away from a wall; keeping
the feet flat on the ground, lower
your body towards the wall,
supporting your weight on your
hands. Hold for 10–15 seconds.

Pelvis, back, hamstring
The hurdler's position. Stretch
out leg, hold ankle with both
hands, lower the head as far as
possible. Repeat three or four
times with each leg alternately,
holding the position for 10–15
seconds each time.

December 1986/January

	COURSE	DISTANCE	TIME hour	min	sec

Monday 29

SLEEP

HEART

WEIGHT

AM

PM

Tuesday 30

SLEEP

HEART

WEIGHT

AM

PM

Wednesday 31

SLEEP

HEART

WEIGHT

AM

PM

Thursday 1

SLEEP

HEART

WEIGHT

AM

PM

Friday 2

SLEEP

HEART

WEIGHT

AM

PM

Saturday 3

SLEEP

HEART

WEIGHT

AM

PM

Sunday 4

SLEEP

HEART

WEIGHT

AM

PM

WEEK'S TOTAL DISTANCE

DESCRIPTION

PERCEIVED
EFFORT   OBSERVATIONS/INJURIES

AM

PM

AM

PM

AM

PM

AM

PM

AM

PM

AM

PM

AM

PM

GENERAL ASSESSMENT

January

	COURSE	DISTANCE	TIME hour	min	sec

Monday 5
SLEEP _____

HEART _____

WEIGHT _____

AM

PM

Tuesday 6
SLEEP _____

HEART _____

WEIGHT _____

AM

PM

Wednesday 7
SLEEP _____

HEART _____

WEIGHT _____

AM

PM

Thursday 8
SLEEP _____

HEART _____

WEIGHT _____

AM

PM

Friday 9
SLEEP _____

HEART _____

WEIGHT _____

AM

PM

Saturday 10
SLEEP _____

HEART _____

WEIGHT _____

AM

PM

Sunday 11
SLEEP _____

HEART _____

WEIGHT _____

AM

PM

WEEK'S TOTAL DISTANCE

DESCRIPTION

PERCEIVED
EFFORT   OBSERVATIONS/INJURIES

AM

PM

AM

PM

AM

PM

AM

PM

AM

PM

AM

PM

AM

PM

GENERAL ASSESSMENT

January

	COURSE	DISTANCE	TIME hour	min	sec

Monday 12
SLEEP

HEART

WEIGHT

AM

PM

Tuesday 13
SLEEP

HEART

WEIGHT

AM

PM

Wednesday 14
SLEEP

HEART

WEIGHT

AM

PM

Thursday 15
SLEEP

HEART

WEIGHT

AM

PM

Friday 16
SLEEP

HEART

WEIGHT

AM

PM

Saturday 17
SLEEP

HEART

WEIGHT

AM

PM

Sunday 18
SLEEP

HEART

WEIGHT

AM

PM

WEEK'S TOTAL DISTANCE

DESCRIPTION

PERCEIVED
EFFORT   OBSERVATIONS/INJURIES

AM

PM

AM

PM

AM

PM

AM

PM

AM

PM

AM

PM

AM

PM

GENERAL ASSESSMENT

January

	COURSE	DISTANCE	TIME hour	min	sec

Monday 19
AM

SLEEP

HEART   PM

WEIGHT

Tuesday 20
AM

SLEEP

HEART   PM

WEIGHT

Wednesday 21
AM

SLEEP

HEART   PM

WEIGHT

Thursday 22
AM

SLEEP

HEART   PM

WEIGHT

Friday 23
AM

SLEEP

HEART   PM

WEIGHT

Saturday 24
AM

SLEEP

HEART   PM

WEIGHT

Sunday 25
AM

SLEEP

HEART   PM

WEIGHT

WEEK'S TOTAL DISTANCE

1987

DESCRIPTION	PERCEIVED EFFORT	OBSERVATIONS/INJURIES

AM

PM

AM

PM

AM

PM

AM

PM

AM

PM

AM

PM

AM

PM

GENERAL ASSESSMENT

January/February

Monday 26
SLEEP _____

HEART _____

WEIGHT _____

AM

PM

Tuesday 27
SLEEP _____

HEART _____

WEIGHT _____

AM

PM

Wednesday 28
SLEEP _____

HEART _____

WEIGHT _____

AM

PM

Thursday 29
SLEEP _____

HEART _____

WEIGHT _____

AM

PM

Friday 30
SLEEP _____

HEART _____

WEIGHT _____

AM

PM

Saturday 31
SLEEP _____

HEART _____

WEIGHT _____

AM

PM

Sunday 1
SLEEP _____

HEART _____

WEIGHT _____

AM

PM

WEEK'S TOTAL DISTANCE _____

DESCRIPTION	PERCEIVED EFFORT	OBSERVATIONS/INJURIES
AM		
PM		
AM		
PM		
AM		
PM		
AM		
PM		
AM		
PM		
AM		
PM		
AM		
PM		

GENERAL ASSESSMENT

February

	COURSE	DISTANCE	TIME hour	min	sec

Monday 2
SLEEP

HEART

WEIGHT

AM

PM

Tuesday 3
SLEEP

HEART

WEIGHT

AM

PM

Wednesday 4
SLEEP

HEART

WEIGHT

AM

PM

Thursday 5
SLEEP

HEART

WEIGHT

AM

PM

Friday 6
SLEEP

HEART

WEIGHT

AM

PM

Saturday 7
SLEEP

HEART

WEIGHT

AM

PM

Sunday 8
SLEEP

HEART

WEIGHT

AM

PM

WEEK'S TOTAL DISTANCE

DESCRIPTION	PERCEIVED EFFORT	OBSERVATIONS/INJURIES
AM		
PM		
AM		
PM		
AM		
PM		
AM		
PM		
AM		
PM		
AM		
PM		
AM		
PM		

GENERAL ASSESSMENT

February

	COURSE	DISTANCE	TIME hour	min	sec

Monday 9
AM

SLEEP

HEART   PM

WEIGHT

Tuesday 10
AM

SLEEP

HEART   PM

WEIGHT

Wednesday 11
AM

SLEEP

HEART   PM

WEIGHT

Thursday 12
AM

SLEEP

HEART   PM

WEIGHT

Friday 13
AM

SLEEP

HEART   PM

WEIGHT

Saturday 14
AM

SLEEP

HEART   PM

WEIGHT

Sunday 15
AM

SLEEP

HEART   PM

WEIGHT

WEEK'S TOTAL DISTANCE

1987

DESCRIPTION

PERCEIVED
EFFORT   OBSERVATIONS/INJURIES

AM

PM

AM

PM

AM

PM

AM

PM

AM

PM

AM

PM

AM

PM

GENERAL ASSESSMENT

February

	COURSE	DISTANCE	TIME hour	min	sec

Monday 16
SLEEP _____
HEART _____
WEIGHT _____

AM

PM

Tuesday 17
SLEEP _____
HEART _____
WEIGHT _____

AM

PM

Wednesday 18
SLEEP _____
HEART _____
WEIGHT _____

AM

PM

Thursday 19
SLEEP _____
HEART _____
WEIGHT _____

AM

PM

Friday 20
SLEEP _____
HEART _____
WEIGHT _____

AM

PM

Saturday 21
SLEEP _____
HEART _____
WEIGHT _____

AM

PM

Sunday 22
SLEEP _____
HEART _____
WEIGHT _____

AM

PM

WEEK'S TOTAL DISTANCE _____

1987

DESCRIPTION	PERCEIVED EFFORT	OBSERVATIONS/INJURIES

AM

PM

AM

PM

AM

PM

AM

PM

AM

PM

AM

PM

AM

PM

GENERAL ASSESSMENT

February/March

	COURSE	DISTANCE	TIME hour	min	sec

Monday 23
SLEEP

HEART

WEIGHT

AM

PM

Tuesday 24
SLEEP

HEART

WEIGHT

AM

PM

Wednesday 25
SLEEP

HEART

WEIGHT

AM

PM

Thursday 26
SLEEP

HEART

WEIGHT

AM

PM

Friday 27
SLEEP

HEART

WEIGHT

AM

PM

Saturday 28
SLEEP

HEART

WEIGHT

AM

PM

Sunday 1
SLEEP

HEART

WEIGHT

AM

PM

WEEK'S TOTAL DISTANCE

DESCRIPTION	PERCEIVED EFFORT	OBSERVATIONS/INJURIES
AM		
PM		
AM		
PM		
AM		
PM		
AM		
PM		
AM		
PM		
AM		
PM		
AM		
PM		

GENERAL ASSESSMENT

March

	COURSE	DISTANCE	TIME hour	min	sec

Monday 2

SLEEP _____

HEART _____

WEIGHT _____

AM

PM

Tuesday 3

SLEEP _____

HEART _____

WEIGHT _____

AM

PM

Wednesday 4

SLEEP _____

HEART _____

WEIGHT _____

AM

PM

Thursday 5

SLEEP _____

HEART _____

WEIGHT _____

AM

PM

Friday 6

SLEEP _____

HEART _____

WEIGHT _____

AM

PM

Saturday 7

SLEEP _____

HEART _____

WEIGHT _____

AM

PM

Sunday 8

SLEEP _____

HEART _____

WEIGHT _____

AM

PM

WEEK'S TOTAL DISTANCE

DESCRIPTION	PERCEIVED EFFORT	OBSERVATIONS/INJURIES
AM		
PM		
AM		
PM		
AM		
PM		
AM		
PM		
AM		
PM		
AM		
PM		
AM		
PM		

GENERAL ASSESSMENT

March

	COURSE	DISTANCE	TIME hour	min	sec

Monday 9
SLEEP

HEART

WEIGHT

AM

PM

Tuesday 10
SLEEP

HEART

WEIGHT

AM

PM

Wednesday 11
SLEEP

HEART

WEIGHT

AM

PM

Thursday 12
SLEEP

HEART

WEIGHT

AM

PM

Friday 13
SLEEP

HEART

WEIGHT

AM

PM

Saturday 14
SLEEP

HEART

WEIGHT

AM

PM

Sunday 15
SLEEP

HEART

WEIGHT

AM

PM

WEEK'S TOTAL DISTANCE

1987

DESCRIPTION	PERCEIVED EFFORT	OBSERVATIONS/INJURIES

AM

PM

AM

PM

AM

PM

AM

PM

AM

PM

AM

PM

AM

PM

GENERAL ASSESSMENT

March

	COURSE	DISTANCE	TIME hour	min	sec

Monday 16
SLEEP _____

HEART _____

WEIGHT _____

AM

PM

Tuesday 17
SLEEP _____

HEART _____

WEIGHT _____

AM

PM

Wednesday 18
SLEEP _____

HEART _____

WEIGHT _____

AM

PM

Thursday 19
SLEEP _____

HEART _____

WEIGHT _____

AM

PM

Friday 20
SLEEP _____

HEART _____

WEIGHT _____

AM

PM

Saturday 21
SLEEP _____

HEART _____

WEIGHT _____

AM

PM

Sunday 22
SLEEP _____

HEART _____

WEIGHT _____

AM

PM

WEEK'S TOTAL DISTANCE

DESCRIPTION	PERCEIVED EFFORT	OBSERVATIONS/INJURIES
AM		
PM		
AM		
PM		
AM		
PM		
AM		
PM		
AM		
PM		
AM		
PM		
AM		
PM		

GENERAL ASSESSMENT

March

	COURSE	DISTANCE	TIME hour	min	sec

Monday 23
SLEEP

HEART

WEIGHT

AM

PM

Tuesday 24
SLEEP

HEART

WEIGHT

AM

PM

Wednesday 25
SLEEP

HEART

WEIGHT

AM

PM

Thursday 26
SLEEP

HEART

WEIGHT

AM

PM

Friday 27
SLEEP

HEART

WEIGHT

AM

PM

Saturday 28
SLEEP

HEART

WEIGHT

AM

PM

Sunday 29
SLEEP

HEART

WEIGHT

AM

PM

WEEK'S TOTAL DISTANCE

DESCRIPTION

PERCEIVED
EFFORT   OBSERVATIONS/INJURIES

AM

PM

AM

PM

AM

PM

AM

PM

AM

PM

AM

PM

AM

PM

GENERAL ASSESSMENT

Marathon time

The business of running a marathon is not something I have got involved with so far, though I feel I would like to have a go at the distance at some stage in the future. But the business of watching a big marathon *is* something I can talk about: I think we've got London Marathon day pretty well sorted out.

I was a bit sceptical when these mass long-distance runs began to catch the public imagination. I had my doubts about the quality of the organisation and whether so many runners would really be catered for properly; it also seemed a fairly inexpensive way for commercial concerns to muscle in on serious athletics. But in almost every case these fears have been unfounded, and after seeing one or two of these early marathons I was thoroughly won over. The sight of so many thousands of men and women running together with a common target is simply unforgettable; whether they are battling towards a personal goal, or forgetting the clock and concentrating on finishing the course, the effort is inspiring, and the extraordinary joy that everyone shows at the finish line is fully deserved.

The spectators themselves are an equally astonishing sight as they pull out all the stops to drive the passing runners forward; one friend of mine, deep in trouble after eighteen miles of the London Marathon, with his resolve melting away, swears he was only persuaded to keep going by a bevy of Folies Bergère girls handing out water and encouragement in the Isle of Dogs.

To see as much of this spirit and courage and goodwill as possible, a marathon spectator at the London needs a bit of imagination and a certain amount of planning. We have a genius in such matters at the Haringey club, and our Marathon Day has become something of a ritual.

We meet, a small bunch of us, near the Monument in the City about an hour before the race is due to start at Blackheath. There we park our cars and dump our unwanted kit, and run slowly across the river and eastwards along the South London streets towards Greenwich and the Cutty Sark. We've run about six miles when we get there, and so have the leading runners, coming at high speed in the opposite direction. There we watch the faster men go past for about five minutes as they race away towards Deptford and Rotherhithe, then we run under the Thames foot-tunnel to the Isle of Dogs and the new Docklands development. At about the fourteen-mile mark we pick up the leaders again, heading towards us from the East End, and then we start trotting slowly along the route in reverse— against the tide, as it were.

It's perfectly possible to do this without getting in the way of the runners, and as long as you don't mind a thousand reminders that 'You're going the wrong way' it's an ideal way of picking out the vests of your club colleagues in the field, or searching for the faces of friends struggling along behind the leaders.

By the time we get close to the Tower of London we are watching runners who are perhaps three-quarters of an hour behind the leaders, maybe more, and who are about half-way through their ordeal. We then run westwards through the City and down towards the Embankment at Charing Cross where the field turns away from the river for that last, exhausting mile-and-a-half of the race. We watch the leaders through there, then we trot back to the City for our tracksuits.

All in all, we will have run about eighteen miles at a fairly leisurely pace while everyone else has run twenty-six miles very hard indeed; we've seen a lot of the race, both at the sharp end and among the strivers further down the field; we've sampled the party atmosphere of the crowds, and we've been greeted, as we have run anti-clockwise through the Isle of Dogs, by a citizen lurching from a pub with the cry: 'Here they come—it's the Irish national marathon squad.' It's a splendid day out. **SC**

The eating runner

What should I eat? The answer for any runner is always, and not very helpfully, 'a well balanced diet'. In everyday terms this means that ordinary, sensible people, unless they are over- or under-weight, can eat pretty well what they like, with very few reservations. Today's highly supplemented foods (just look at the ingredients listed on your margarine or your cornflakes packet), together with fresh fruit, lightly cooked vegetables and a glass of milk will ensure that your diet contains all the essentials you will need. This is not an encouragement to eat rubbish, but there is no need to force down something you do not enjoy when there is such a wide range of food from which to choose your balanced diet.

How much should I eat? A medium-active man weighing 70kg (about 11 stone) needs around 2,900 Calories per day. To this a runner must add the energy requirements for training. In broad terms, depending on your overall efficiency, running at a pace of 6 minutes 30 seconds per mile could burn up around 18–20 Calories per minute.

A rough-and-ready adjustment for different body weights involves adding or subtracting ten per cent of the daily Calorie requirement for each 7kg (15lb) above or below the 70kg. If you are feeling tired and/or losing weight, first check your diet. A weight gain will be equally telltale, but the right balance will keep your weight constant and help to keep you feeling well.

What about proportions? Now you're getting technical, but we would suggest the following:

NUTRIENT	PERCENTAGE OF DIET	CALORIES	CALORIES PER GRAM	WEIGHT OF FOOD*
Protein	15	435	4	= 109 grams (3.84oz)
Fat	25	725	9	= 80 grams (2.82oz)
Carbohydrate	60	1740	4	= 435 grams (15.34oz)
Total	100	2900		= 624 grams (22.0 oz)

*Actual substance. This is the yield of a fat or a protein from the food, which will, of course, contain water, fibre etc.

This should ensure enough protein for growth and tissue replacement and the essential amino-acids; enough fat to yield energy (twice as much as in carbohydrates, so watch it) and essential fatty acids which are best obtained from vegetable oils and fats; and plenty of carbohydrates for quicker energy.

The following meal yields about 1,000 Calories, and would supply approximately half your daily mineral and vitamin needs (calcium 43%, iron 58%, thiamin 46%, riboflavin 42% and all nicotinic acid and vitamin C. The missing vitamin D would come from an ounce of margarine with other meals).

	WEIGHT	CALORIES	PROTEIN (G)	FAT (G)	CARBOHYDRATE (G)
Orange juice	(large glass)	120	1.2	0	28.8
Steak & kidney pie	5oz (142g)	413.6	21.5	26.0	23.0
Boiled peas	3oz (85g)	32.4	4.5	0	3.6
Roast potatoes	6oz (170g)	279.6	4.8	8.4	46.2
Tinned peaches	4oz (113g)	105.6	0.4	0	26.0
Custard	3oz (85g)	103.2	3.3	3.6	14.4
Total		1054.4	35.7	38.0	142.0
Conversion (Calories per gram)			x4	x9	x4
Total Calories in meal		1054.4	142.8	342.0	569.6
(percentages)		(100%)	(13.5%)	(32.4%)	(54.0%)

This is not exactly the 15–25–60 ratio suggested on page 53, but there will be two or possibly three more meals that day in which you can adjust. In any case, under normal cooking conditions you will not be conducting exact scientific experiments.

A few words about 'essentials'. They are those minerals and vitamins that the body cannot manufacture for itself. As has already been said, you are unlikely to suffer from vitamin deficiency, and supplements are expensive — but personal experience has convinced us of the value of some additional vitamin C and iron supplement during heavy training. Vitamin C is helpful in aiding body repairs and combating illness, and runners may lose more iron than other people when the red cells break up at the end of their three-to-four-month life.

The following table shows how easily the main vitamins are obtained:

VITAMIN	SOURCE	DEFICIENCY SYMPTOMS
A	Milk, butter, liver, cod liver oil, fresh green vegetables	Lowered resistance to illness, bad skin
B	Wheat germ, yeast	Lack of appetite, indigestion, wasting
B complex	Wheat germ, yeast, nuts, fish, meat, milk products	Lack of appetite, indigestion, wasting
C	Fresh green vegetables, citrus fruits	Scurvy, lowered resistance, poor healing
D complex	Cod liver oil, eggs, cream	Poor bones (e.g. rickets)

As we have said, supplements are not usually necessary, but some authorities do advocate vitamin supplements during the heaviest part of the training, and a check that your full vitamin requirements are being met is certainly worthwhile if you are on a 70-mile-per-week schedule that includes hard speed endurance. Of those national coaching organisations recommending an extra vitamin intake, the Russians exceed even the Finns and the Canadians. Their recommendation for endurance events during hard training is as follows:

Vitamin	A	B_1	B_2	Ncn	C	E
Milligrams per day	3	10	5	25	250	6

Such an intake would do no harm to anyone in hard training, but at the same time it would be quite useless to anyone else. **PC**

Running at grass roots

In my last year as a junior, madly keen and anxious to get more competition, I entered the 1500 metres in the Yorkshire championships, early in the season. Walter Wilkinson was the Yorkshire star in those days, towards the end of his fine international career. He was in the 1500 metres, too, tuning up for the rigours of another heavy season to come. I was a bit green, I suppose; I'm sure I didn't fully realise what I was doing in the race; I was unknown, and I had absolutely nothing to lose. As luck would have it I had enough left at the end to get up and pass Walter in the final straight.

Athletics has a sneaky way of turning the tables on you. A few years later, early in 1981, I went back to the Yorkshire championships for the first 800 metres of what was going to be an important year. This time I suppose that it was I who was the star, but I was chiefly looking for a pleasant early-season outing to test the winter's training. I got to the 600-metre mark to find every step dogged by a young red-headed lad from Rotherham who was only shaken off by some desperate late sprinting from me. That was Peter Elliott announcing his arrival.

It's little incidents like those that make you realise where the real giant-killing takes place. In an Olympic Games or a World Championship an unfancied runner might have an exceptional day and even beat the favourite in the final, but he won't exactly be an unknown. At a club or a county meeting, though, a young runner who is literally unknown to the title-holder can turn the form-book upside-down. Walter Wilkinson, I'm sure, will have had his own days as a raw young runner worrying a champion like Alan Simpson, and Alan probably had his own tilt at Derek Ibbotson.

Athletics at this grassroots level gives benefit to everybody. At the start of each season I can use these reasonably relaxed affairs to gauge my own fitness. For the young club athlete, as we have seen, a couple of international runners in the field can prove more of an incentive than any amount of pre-season training. And the chance of seeing a local star back at the local track can bring in enough spectators to give even a minor meeting a real sense of occasion.

It was the strength of club athletics that enabled runners like me to reach the international stage. It is at club level that the vast bulk of talented athletes and coaches operate, and it would have been quite impossible for me to win major races in those early years without the advice of my clubmates and their coaches.

And today, after nearly ten years of international running, the most enjoyable parts of my running year are those that involve my Haringey club—the winter training runs, the club road relays on the streets of London, the occasional 3,000 metres in front of six spectators and a dog. Away from the limelight, sharing other people's successes and failures, enjoying a pint and a bag of crisps and just being part of a living athletics community is not just a vital part of my running life—it's also very enjoyable.   **SC**

Aiming for a fun run

If you feel that you're ready to test out your new-found running ability in public, why not try a fun run? The fun run is one of the more curious developments of the running boom—a race over a set course, but one in which you are not expected to be competitive. In any fun run, make no mistake, there will be people racing for all they are worth, but for every serious competitor there will be dozens just running along at their own pace in a friendly group. Racing is serious, fun-running is not—though many fun-runners have gone on to racing and enjoyed that too.

Let us presume that you are not yet what you would call a serious runner, but that you would like to take part in a real event. There are only three rules:

1. Put aside your natural anxiety; you cannot be 'shown up' in a fun run.
2. Make sure before you start that you can comfortably complete the distance.

3. Do not run so hard that you become unobservant during your run. It will probably be your first experience of running en masse on public roads, and there is a lot to learn, including what *not* to do, by looking at other people.

Preparation   Let us assume it is a three-mile run. And let us also assume you have done at least some jogging and some running, perhaps as much as in our 'First Steps' programme (page 14). If so, you will already have run in excess of three miles, so you will have to do no more than run steadily, inside your best pace.

Most likely the course will be posted well before the day. If so, you will get more enjoyment out of the run if you go round the course a couple of times to assess your most comfortable pace.

Even if you have not completed our First Steps schedule, so long as you are moderately fit you can shorten our preparation by curtailing each stage of the steps, for example by cutting the one-hour stages to half-an-hour each. And if by the time of the fun run you are still jogging rather than running, then jog the fun run. Don't get carried away and stride out. You should finish your fun run wanting to do it again, not put off for ever.

The run   In general, the usual race rules apply. Wear comfortable, broken-in running shoes (not gym shoes or plimsolls), shorts and vest and socks you are used to, all clean and dried. Tie your laces properly. (Don't laugh; your bending down to re-tie a shoelace may be hilarious for the onlookers, but in a large field with everyone running over you it could take all the fun out of your fun run.)

If the event is well supported, you will probably shuffle off in the middle of the pack and not find much space for quite a while. The only really clear space in any run, Olympic final or mass fun run, is either right at the front or right at the back; if you get stuck in the middle, just relax and enjoy it.

Finally, if the run is on public roads, obey the rules of the marshals, and do keep an eye open for traffic. Safety first at all times.   **PC**

The athlete as promoter

It was the longest, most tiring day of athletics I've ever spent in my life—not because of my race, which had been hard but fairly routine, but because I'd spent most of the meeting on the other side of the fence; I had organised it.

It was the first Loughborough v AAA meeting, back in 1983. The university was celebrating its fiftieth anniversary, and it had recently laid down a new running track, so an athletics get-together with a sprinkling of top-class names seemed an ideal way of marking both events. And I was asked to get it all together. The idea was fine, the permission to stage it was readily given by the AAA—all we had to do was book the athletes, publicise the event, make sure we didn't make a loss and see that the day went smoothly ... the sort of thing that happens dozens of times each season throughout the country. Easy, we thought.

The central problem is always the same. The meeting needed a sponsor to bear the majority of the costs. The potential sponsor would only be interested if the meeting were to be televised. The television people would only say yes if the standard of athletics was going to be high. And top-class athletes are the hardest sportsmen of all to pin down to a date six months in advance.

The negotiations took weeks—phone calls, meetings, trips to London and back, begging, persuading, arm-twisting ... but eventually it all fell into place: the athletes said yes, TV gave the go-ahead, the sponsor came up with the money and all we had to do, it seemed, was to pray for a sunny Sunday.

Then came one of those little niggles which seem utterly insignificant in retrospect, but which at the time seemed a potential disaster: Margaret Thatcher called a general election for the Thursday before our meeting. Hardly a problem in itself, except that all our tickets and posters were emblazoned with the announcement that the meeting would be opened 'by Neil Macfarlane MP, Minister for Sport'. The closer the meeting came, the greater our awareness that if the Conservatives got into difficulties, we were faced with a major embarrassment. Neil Macfarlane might, it was perfectly possible, not be an MP by that crucial Sunday; even if he were re-elected, he might well not be minister for sport, or minister for anything else, for that matter. As things turned out, we needn't have worried, but it was yet another thing to keep us biting our nails.

Then came the day itself. Normally on the morning of a race I would have a leisurely breakfast after getting up late, and wander round the house reading the papers; on that day I was out on the track by 7.30, sorting out camera angles with the television production team and arranging the final commentary positions, making sure that the banners were in the right positions, answering last-minute queries about the site of the portaloos and the ice-cream concessions and the placing of the sponsor's tents. We're all very pleased, I'm sure, that these details are all relevant to modern athletics, but they're something of a drain on your time and patience if you are the one responsible for them all.

Suddenly it was two-thirty in the afternoon, with half-an-hour left for a quick change into running kit and a high-speed warm-up before my own race at my own meeting ... and a fervent wish that I hadn't been quite so successful at persuading such an accomplished field of 800-metre runners to come and compete against us—the last thing I wanted at that stage of the day was a tough race.

It *was* a tough race, but I had enough energy left to hold on to win it ... only to find myself stepping off the track to deal with all the press requirements before I could get back to checking that the sponsor was still happy and the tents were still standing and that the drinks hadn't run out.

The athletics finished at seven o'clock. At nine we were still seeing people off the premises, and next morning we began winding up all the correspondence, making sure the runners' expenses had been paid, looking for kit that people had rung up to report lost. . . .

The athletes had all competed without a fee, and the people of Loughborough had given their time and effort with tremendous generosity. There had been seven thousand satisfied customers, it hadn't rained, and there was a real feeling of satisfaction that six months' planning and hard work had been well rewarded and that a repeat performance was already in hand for the following year. For me it provided a remarkable insight into the problems that all organisers must face—but once a year is quite enough. **SC**

Legs and feet

Many athletics injuries originate from the way runners misuse their feet. Nature developed our feet to run on natural terrain, but we are forced to do most, if not all, of our running on rock-hard surfaces. Shoes are therefore at best a compromise, and they can easily contribute to our troubles if they are not chosen wisely, particularly as they will almost certainly represent any runner's biggest single item of expenditure.

We suggest you consider all the following criteria when you are choosing your shoes:

Protection from shock: Support for the intricate structure of the foot, and particularly a firm counter for the heel.

Toe-off flexibility: While the arch must be properly supported, the shoe must bend easily under the ball of the foot without the folds cutting into the top of the foot.

Stability: The sole must act as a cushion, but not be so mushy as to prevent the foot from feeling firm on the ground; it should not allow too much rocking and rolling.

Arch support: Should give a full ground contact; the shoe should not be cut away under the arch.

Weight: Less important than good design. Lighter is not necessarily faster.

Traction: The shoe must provide a good grip on the surface you expect to run on.

Uppers: Leather lasts longer and is cooler, but it is heavy when wet. Nylon is softer and needs little if any breaking-in; a good nylon mesh will help to make a cooler shoe.

Tongue: Must give protection from the pressure of the laces and not wander around when you're running.

Lacing: Should have an eyelet arrangement that allows for different lacing patterns.

Inside: No irritating seams, high or 'hot' spots. The box must protect the toes. The insoles must not move or wrinkle.

Finally, beware of gimmicks like very high heel tabs and over-cushioned ankle pads that only rub and irritate.

Good shoes are important, but don't forget the feet that go inside them.

- Keep your feet clean.
- Keep your toe-nails properly trimmed (not growing in at the corners).
- Keep hard patches of skin thinned down. Skin thickens to give protection to weak spots, but if it is allowed to thicken too much it cracks, and these cracks are difficult to heal. Even worse, if a blister forms under very thick skin, it will create a very raw patch indeed.
- Corns should be treated before they become too deep and, more important, the cause should be found and eliminated.

Foot care includes, where necessary, wearing the correct orthotics. Correcting any imbalance, any structural fault, is very important, and to this end the modern, very light and rigid type of orthotic insert can work miracles. Many leg problems, too, can originate in the feet, since the stability of many joints is influenced by the strength of the related muscles. So regular exercises for the feet can be of benefit—for example:

- Roll a ball or a bottle around under the foot with varying pressure.
- Do heel-raises with a book or block under the ball of the foot.
- Do 'pick-up' exercises with the toes. Practise picking up small objects like thimbles and pencils.
- Develop gripping power of the toes by squeezing, and by trying to lift heavy objects.

We warm up to improve our performance, yet so many runners allow their legs to cool off, or even to get cold, at track and cross-country meetings. Unless it is a really warm day, keep your legs covered and protected when you are not running or training hard.

Do plenty of flexibility exercises, and remember that wobble-board exercise is good for the feet and ankles. Serious runners should consider the benefits of regular and properly applied massage.

DO NOT run through any pain or discomfort in the legs or the feet. Stop, and find out what the cause is. The achilles tendon and the knees are common sites of injury. Never ignore any symptoms, and if with normal care and treatment the trouble does not clear up quickly, see a physiotherapist or a *sports-minded* doctor.

For the sake of your legs and feet, do not run in worn-down or rolled-over shoes. And don't forget that stretching, heel-raising and quadriceps exercises can be done frequently, if briefly, throughout the day in most jobs.   **PC**

March/April

	COURSE	DISTANCE	TIME hour	min	sec

Monday 30
AM

SLEEP _____

HEART _____ PM

WEIGHT _____

Tuesday 31
AM

SLEEP _____

HEART _____ PM

WEIGHT _____

Wednesday 1
AM

SLEEP _____

HEART _____ PM

WEIGHT _____

Thursday 2
AM

SLEEP _____

HEART _____ PM

WEIGHT _____

Friday 3
AM

SLEEP _____

HEART _____ PM

WEIGHT _____

Saturday 4
AM

SLEEP _____

HEART _____ PM

WEIGHT _____

Sunday 5
AM

SLEEP _____

HEART _____ PM

WEIGHT _____

WEEK'S TOTAL DISTANCE

1987

DESCRIPTION	PERCEIVED EFFORT	OBSERVATIONS/INJURIES

AM

_____   _____

PM

AM

_____   _____

PM

AM

_____   _____

PM

AM

_____   _____

PM

AM

_____   _____

PM

AM

_____   _____

PM

AM

_____   _____

PM

GENERAL ASSESSMENT

April

	COURSE	DISTANCE	TIME hour	min	sec

Monday 6
SLEEP _____

HEART _____

WEIGHT _____

AM _____

PM _____

Tuesday 7
SLEEP _____

HEART _____

WEIGHT _____

AM _____

PM _____

Wednesday 8
SLEEP _____

HEART _____

WEIGHT _____

AM _____

PM _____

Thursday 9
SLEEP _____

HEART _____

WEIGHT _____

AM _____

PM _____

Friday 10
SLEEP _____

HEART _____

WEIGHT _____

AM _____

PM _____

Saturday 11
SLEEP _____

HEART _____

WEIGHT _____

AM _____

PM _____

Sunday 12
SLEEP _____

HEART _____

WEIGHT _____

AM _____

PM _____

WEEK'S TOTAL DISTANCE _____

1987

DESCRIPTION	PERCEIVED EFFORT	OBSERVATIONS/INJURIES
AM		
PM		
AM		
PM		
AM		
PM		
AM		
PM		
AM		
PM		
AM		
PM		
AM		
PM		

GENERAL ASSESSMENT

April

	COURSE	DISTANCE	TIME hour	min	sec

Monday 13
SLEEP _____

HEART _____

WEIGHT _____

AM

PM

Tuesday 14
SLEEP _____

HEART _____

WEIGHT _____

AM

PM

Wednesday 15
SLEEP _____

HEART _____

WEIGHT _____

AM

PM

Thursday 16
SLEEP _____

HEART _____

WEIGHT _____

AM

PM

Friday 17
SLEEP _____

HEART _____

WEIGHT _____

AM

PM

Saturday 18
SLEEP _____

HEART _____

WEIGHT _____

AM

PM

Sunday 19
SLEEP _____

HEART _____

WEIGHT _____

AM

PM

WEEK'S TOTAL DISTANCE

DESCRIPTION	PERCEIVED EFFORT	OBSERVATIONS/INJURIES
AM		
PM		
AM		
PM		
AM		
PM		
AM		
PM		
AM		
PM		
AM		
PM		
AM		
PM		

GENERAL ASSESSMENT

April

	COURSE	DISTANCE	TIME hour	min	sec

Monday 20

SLEEP

HEART

WEIGHT

AM

PM

Tuesday 21

SLEEP

HEART

WEIGHT

AM

PM

Wednesday 22

SLEEP

HEART

WEIGHT

AM

PM

Thursday 23

SLEEP

HEART

WEIGHT

AM

PM

Friday 24

SLEEP

HEART

WEIGHT

AM

PM

Saturday 25

SLEEP

HEART

WEIGHT

AM

PM

Sunday 26

SLEEP

HEART

WEIGHT

AM

PM

WEEK'S TOTAL DISTANCE

1987

DESCRIPTION	PERCEIVED EFFORT	OBSERVATIONS/INJURIES
AM		
PM		
AM		
PM		
AM		
PM		
AM		
PM		
AM		
PM		
AM		
PM		
AM		
PM		

GENERAL ASSESSMENT

April/May

	COURSE	DISTANCE	TIME hour	min	sec

Monday 27
SLEEP ___

HEART ___

WEIGHT ___

AM

PM

Tuesday 28
SLEEP ___

HEART ___

WEIGHT ___

AM

PM

Wednesday 29
SLEEP ___

HEART ___

WEIGHT ___

AM

PM

Thursday 30
SLEEP ___

HEART ___

WEIGHT ___

AM

PM

Friday 1
SLEEP ___

HEART ___

WEIGHT ___

AM

PM

Saturday 2
SLEEP ___

HEART ___

WEIGHT ___

AM

PM

Sunday 3
SLEEP ___

HEART ___

WEIGHT ___

AM

PM

WEEK'S TOTAL DISTANCE

DESCRIPTION	PERCEIVED EFFORT	OBSERVATIONS/INJURIES
AM		
PM		
AM		
PM		
AM		
PM		
AM		
PM		
AM		
PM		
AM		
PM		
AM		
PM		

GENERAL ASSESSMENT

May

	COURSE	DISTANCE	TIME hour	min	sec

Monday 4
SLEEP

HEART

WEIGHT

AM

PM

Tuesday 5
SLEEP

HEART

WEIGHT

AM

PM

Wednesday 6
SLEEP

HEART

WEIGHT

AM

PM

Thursday 7
SLEEP

HEART

WEIGHT

AM

PM

Friday 8
SLEEP

HEART

WEIGHT

AM

PM

Saturday 9
SLEEP

HEART

WEIGHT

AM

PM

Sunday 10
SLEEP

HEART

WEIGHT

AM

PM

WEEK'S TOTAL DISTANCE

DESCRIPTION	PERCEIVED EFFORT	OBSERVATIONS/INJURIES

AM

_____   _____

PM

AM

_____   _____

PM

AM

_____   _____

PM

AM

_____   _____

PM

AM

_____   _____

PM

AM

_____   _____

PM

AM

_____   _____

PM

GENERAL ASSESSMENT

May

	COURSE	DISTANCE	TIME hour	min	sec

Monday 11

SLEEP

HEART

WEIGHT

AM

PM

Tuesday 12

SLEEP

HEART

WEIGHT

AM

PM

Wednesday 13

SLEEP

HEART

WEIGHT

AM

PM

Thursday 14

SLEEP

HEART

WEIGHT

AM

PM

Friday 15

SLEEP

HEART

WEIGHT

AM

PM

Saturday 16

SLEEP

HEART

WEIGHT

AM

PM

Sunday 17

SLEEP

HEART

WEIGHT

AM

PM

WEEK'S TOTAL DISTANCE

DESCRIPTION	PERCEIVED EFFORT	OBSERVATIONS/INJURIES
AM		
PM		
AM		
PM		
AM		
PM		
AM		
PM		
AM		
PM		
AM		
PM		
AM		
PM		

GENERAL ASSESSMENT

May

	COURSE	DISTANCE	TIME hour	min	sec

Monday 18
SLEEP

HEART

WEIGHT

AM

PM

Tuesday 19
SLEEP

HEART

WEIGHT

AM

PM

Wednesday 20
SLEEP

HEART

WEIGHT

AM

PM

Thursday 21
SLEEP

HEART

WEIGHT

AM

PM

Friday 22
SLEEP

HEART

WEIGHT

AM

PM

Saturday 23
SLEEP

HEART

WEIGHT

AM

PM

Sunday 24
SLEEP

HEART

WEIGHT

AM

PM

WEEK'S TOTAL DISTANCE

1987

DESCRIPTION

PERCEIVED
EFFORT   OBSERVATIONS/INJURIES

AM

PM

AM

PM

AM

PM

AM

PM

AM

PM

AM

PM

AM

PM

GENERAL ASSESSMENT

May

	COURSE		DISTANCE	TIME hour	min	sec

Monday 25
SLEEP _____

HEART _____

WEIGHT _____

AM

PM

Tuesday 26
SLEEP _____

HEART _____

WEIGHT _____

AM

PM

Wednesday 27
SLEEP _____

HEART _____

WEIGHT _____

AM

PM

Thursday 28
SLEEP _____

HEART _____

WEIGHT _____

AM

PM

Friday 29
SLEEP _____

HEART _____

WEIGHT _____

AM

PM

Saturday 30
SLEEP _____

HEART _____

WEIGHT _____

AM

PM

Sunday 31
SLEEP _____

HEART _____

WEIGHT _____

AM

PM

WEEK'S TOTAL DISTANCE _____

DESCRIPTION	PERCEIVED EFFORT	OBSERVATIONS/INJURIES
AM		
PM		
AM		
PM		
AM		
PM		
AM		
PM		
AM		
PM		
AM		
PM		
AM		
PM		

GENERAL ASSESSMENT

June

Monday 1

SLEEP _____

HEART _____

WEIGHT _____

AM _____ _____ _____ _____ _____

PM _____

Tuesday 2

SLEEP _____

HEART _____

WEIGHT _____

AM _____ _____ _____ _____ _____

PM _____

Wednesday 3

SLEEP _____

HEART _____

WEIGHT _____

AM _____ _____ _____ _____ _____

PM _____

Thursday 4

SLEEP _____

HEART _____

WEIGHT _____

AM _____ _____ _____ _____ _____

PM _____

Friday 5

SLEEP _____

HEART _____

WEIGHT _____

AM _____ _____ _____ _____ _____

PM _____

Saturday 6

SLEEP _____

HEART _____

WEIGHT _____

AM _____ _____ _____ _____ _____

PM _____

Sunday 7

SLEEP _____

HEART _____

WEIGHT _____

AM _____ _____ _____ _____ _____

PM _____

WEEK'S TOTAL DISTANCE _____

DESCRIPTION	PERCEIVED EFFORT	OBSERVATIONS/INJURIES
AM		
PM		
AM		
PM		
AM		
PM		
AM		
PM		
AM		
PM		
AM		
PM		
AM		
PM		

GENERAL ASSESSMENT

June

	COURSE	DISTANCE	TIME hour	min	sec

Monday 8
SLEEP _____

HEART _____

WEIGHT _____

AM

PM

Tuesday 9
SLEEP _____

HEART _____

WEIGHT _____

AM

PM

Wednesday 10
SLEEP _____

HEART _____

WEIGHT _____

AM

PM

Thursday 11
SLEEP _____

HEART _____

WEIGHT _____

AM

PM

Friday 12
SLEEP _____

HEART _____

WEIGHT _____

AM

PM

Saturday 13
SLEEP _____

HEART _____

WEIGHT _____

AM

PM

Sunday 14
SLEEP _____

HEART _____

WEIGHT _____

AM

PM

WEEK'S TOTAL DISTANCE _____

DESCRIPTION	PERCEIVED EFFORT	OBSERVATIONS·INJURIES
AM		
PM		
AM		
PM		
AM		
PM		
AM		
PM		
AM		
PM		
AM		
PM		
AM		
PM		

GENERAL ASSESSMENT

June

Monday 15

SLEEP _____

HEART _____

WEIGHT _____

AM

PM

Tuesday 16

SLEEP _____

HEART _____

WEIGHT _____

AM

PM

Wednesday 17

SLEEP _____

HEART _____

WEIGHT _____

AM

PM

Thursday 18

SLEEP _____

HEART _____

WEIGHT _____

AM

PM

Friday 19

SLEEP _____

HEART _____

WEIGHT _____

AM

PM

Saturday 20

SLEEP _____

HEART _____

WEIGHT _____

AM

PM

Sunday 21

SLEEP _____

HEART _____

WEIGHT _____

AM

PM

WEEK'S TOTAL DISTANCE

DESCRIPTION	PERCEIVED EFFORT	OBSERVATIONS/INJURIES

AM

_____   _____

PM

AM

_____   _____

PM

AM

_____   _____

PM

AM

_____   _____

PM

AM

_____   _____

PM

AM

_____   _____

PM

AM

_____   _____

PM

GENERAL ASSESSMENT

June

	COURSE	DISTANCE	TIME hour	min	sec

Monday 22
SLEEP

HEART

WEIGHT

AM

PM

Tuesday 23
SLEEP

HEART

WEIGHT

AM

PM

Wednesday 24
SLEEP

HEART

WEIGHT

AM

PM

Thursday 25
SLEEP

HEART

WEIGHT

AM

PM

Friday 26
SLEEP

HEART

WEIGHT

AM

PM

Saturday 27
SLEEP

HEART

WEIGHT

AM

PM

Sunday 28
SLEEP

HEART

WEIGHT

AM

PM

WEEK'S TOTAL DISTANCE

1987

DESCRIPTION	PERCEIVED EFFORT	OBSERVATIONS/INJURIES

AM

_____ _____

PM

AM

_____ _____

PM

AM

_____ _____

PM

AM

_____ _____

PM

AM

_____ _____

PM

AM

_____ _____

PM

AM

_____ _____

PM

GENERAL ASSESSMENT

Fit for the start

You learn to appreciate the warm-up and its value if for some reason you are prevented from doing it properly one day. I remember a road relay a couple of winters ago; I was driving up to Birmingham to meet the rest of the Haringey team, and horrific reports on the radio about tailbacks on the motorway persuaded me to try the scenic route through Oxford and Warwick and seemingly all points west and east. Which meant that by the time I got to the venue at Sutton Coldfield there was less than half an hour to the start. I was stiff from the long drive, I had no time to relax with a cup of tea, and barely the chance to get changed and go through a rudimentary warm-up. Needless to say, I didn't run as well as I should have done.

A good warm-up has a genuine psychological effect, as well as the obvious physical one, and the proper preparation for a race is as far removed as possible you can imagine from that panic at Sutton Coldfield. All the big stadiums have pretty good facilities these days — grass areas away from the noise and the lights of the track — and once you are there you can dampen down the nerves. It's good to know, once you've started your routine, that you have somehow got into the first act of the race.

It's a chance to catch a glimpse of the other athletes, too. We all seem to be giving each other sideways glances, just to check up on who's there. But really you are concentrating on your own warm-up, you haven't a lot of time to look at theirs. Even if you did you wouldn't learn much — they're unlikely actually to be limping, or anything like that.

I think some athletes are inclined to overdo the warm-up — perhaps because of nervousness. You have to remember that a warm-up is principally to warm you up, and if you can add to that a bit of suppleness and freedom of movement there is no need to go on flogging yourself for an hour or an hour-and-a-half. Some people have almost completed a full training session by the time they walk out on to the track — it can't do a lot for their performance.

On a reasonably warm evening, I would never need more than thirty-five to forty minutes. The sequence I use has taken shape over the years; I didn't sit down and map it out, it has evolved gradually into its present shape, and it works physically and mentally for me. It gets me to the start line warm, supple and psychologically prepared for what I have come to do. This is roughly what I do:

- Alternately walk and jog for five minutes or so.
- Jog continuously at a slightly quicker pace for another five minutes, slipping in the occasional high knee-lift and short burst of fast-cadence steps, something like a

sprinter's speed drill. By now I am warm enough for stretching.

- Static-stretch calves and hamstrings, slowly stretching one leg at a time by leaning forward against a wall or stanchion with the hands and the leading leg ready to take the weight and control the tension, the rear leg being stretched with the heel firmly on the ground.
- Loosen up the neck, shoulders and arms; combined leg and trunk stretching, by alternately placing first one straight leg and then the other, raised nearly horizontal, on to a radiator, a chair or a low wall, then bending the trunk forward as parallel as possible with the raised leg and placing the head on the raised knee.
- Stand legs astride, hands on hips or behind the head; bend and rotate the trunk.
- Follow with a few half-squats, remembering the static part—holding each position for 10–15 seconds. I would allow 8–10 minutes for the stretching exercises.
- Resume jogging which, as soon as any 'stretched' feeling passes off, turns into steady running. By now I am warmed up.
- Then a set of, say, four fast-striding runs over about 60 metres each.
- Jog down for half a minute. And that's it.

The whole routine is timed to finish as close to the start of the event as possible. I stay well wrapped up throughout.   SC

The warm-up....

Every work-out should be preceded by a warm-up. Why? To prepare you physically and mentally for training or competition. First, it enables you to perform better (as much as five per cent improvement has been shown in 800-metre times as the difference between running after a warm-up and running without one). Secondly, particularly in cold weather, it considerably reduces the risk of injury.

Your object is to raise the core temperature of the body, that is to say the actual temperature of the working muscles, and to dilate the blood vessels supplying them. The cells of the human body work faster at higher temperatures, and the oxygen up-take from the blood to the body tissues is also faster. In addition, and this is of particular interest to sprinters and athletes in explosive events, nerve messages also travel much faster when the body is warmed up. Warm tissue and muscles move more freely, too—the stiffness you feel when you are cold is much more severe than when you are warm. And if that was not enough evidence, ECG tests have found that without a prior warm-up, strenuous exercise produced heart-rhythm abnormalities in *sixty per cent* of the people tested, none of whom otherwise showed any symptoms; after a two-minute warm-up, the same test revealed no abnormalities at all.

The aim is a rise of 1 degree C in the body's core temperature, or deep inner temperature (to distinguish it from the warmth felt, say, on the forehead after 'working up a sweat'). And, unfortunately for the lazy ones, experiments have proved that a passive warm-up, like a hot bath or a sauna, is far less effective than an exercise warm-up.

The duration and intensity of any warm-up depends on the nature of the training session or the race. We recommend commencing with a slow jog and slowly increasing the pace to a steady striding. When you are feeling a lot looser and warmer, pause for your static stretching exercises, then continue with steady running, occasionally breaking into fast strides over twenty or thirty paces, and mixing this with light callisthenics between runs.

Much depends upon the temperature and the environment, indoors or outdoors, summer or winter. When outdoors in winter, try to warm up sheltered from the wind, and in very bad weather take as much shelter and protection as you can to avoid long, tiring warm-ups. In summer, warm-ups are usually quicker and easier.

What is very important is that the actual racing or training should follow as closely as possible on the warm-up. This is not always easy at the big track meetings, but it is advisable that not more than fifteen minutes should elapse between warm-up and strenuous work, and you should keep well covered until the start.

However many distance training runs you may begin without a warm-up (and you are at no great risk if you are well clad or it is a warm spring or summer day, and if you make it a rule to start slowly and build up gradually to your training pace), warm-ups are always absolutely necessary before any speed training, and must never be missed. If you arrive late for squad training (a crime in itself) do not join in straight away−warm up first. It is better to miss a session than to risk injury.

Once you have settled on your warm-up routine, stick to it−it is good for your confidence to know that you have completed a good routine prior to performing. The duration of the warm-up period varies from runner to runner; some athletes take an hour or more before big events, but others perform well after far less. Seb describes his routine on page 95.

As in all aspects of training, do only enough to achieve the purpose. Warm-up time, like mileage, is not necessarily better for being longer and harder. For most beginners, joggers, and runners who are not proceeding to a hard work-out, ten minutes is probably enough.

....and the warm-down

Just as every work-out should be preceded by a warm-up, so it should be followed by a warm-down — to help avoid stiffness and to speed up the replenishment of glycogen.

After hard exercise, especially prolonged hard exercise, there is an increase in intracapillary blood pressure which causes an increase in the intracellular fluid. It is presumed that this is due to the development of acidosis in the muscle cell. Lactate accumulation affects performance and delays recovery, so it is best got rid of as soon as possible. And this is not helped by stopping running and shutting off the muscle pump suddenly, thus reducing circulation.

The muscle pump works on the lymphatic network, which also plays its own part in clearing the muscle. If you start the 'intense' phase of your warm-down without stopping after the hard training, these waste products can be removed in something like thirty minutes; if the warm-down is neglected, it can take anything from two to four hours.

The by-products are most rapidly re-absorbed if the warm-down phase is carried out at a speed sufficient to produce a level of VO_2 uptake of 70 per cent of maximum. (It is just possible that you won't be carrying around equipment to measure VO_2 uptake — the rough equivalent in heart rate would be around 145 per minute for men, 160 per minute for women.)

Immediately your training run finishes, without stopping running, maintain this faster phase of the warm-down for about six minutes, and then jog slowly until you are fully recovered. Alternatively, six minutes before the end of your long hard run, reduce your pace to the fast-phase level, and then complete the warm-down at the end of your run with a jog.

A warm-down is not necessary after a long slow steady run, but it is a must after speed or speed endurance sessions, or after hard hill sessions. **PC**

Days in the village

August is championship time—Commonwealth, European, World, Olympic. For anyone who has taken part in one of these great festivals, memories of late summer always seem to merge with memories of athletes' villages—of communal meals, shared bedrooms, the jumbles of other people's kit and growing excitement as competition day draws near.

If you can cope with life in the village, you can probably expect to perform at your best when you finally get on to the track; but for a lot of people it isn't that easy. In some ways one's capacity for dealing with village life is directly related to the structure of one's normal day. If, in common with so many athletes today, a normal day is spent trying to find things to do between training sessions and meals, then you're going to feel very much at home in an Olympic village.

However, an athlete used to a structured day, a runner who is also meeting the schedules of a nine-to-five job or fitting his training round the demands of a family, is going to need a lot of character to come to terms with the village. To wake up every morning, from the time you arrive to the time of your race, knowing that there is absolutely nothing that you have *got* to do except fit in a couple of training sessions and three meals, can become a real burden. I've seen a lot of runners whose performances have suffered precisely because of this apparent freedom.

You barely have to think in one of these villages. Training is so convenient that you don't even have to make your customary humdrum arrangements for travelling to a session: the track is probably no more than 200 yards from the door of your room. As for the meals, they're available round the clock, excellently prepared, as much as you want completely free of charge—in the Olympic canteen it's Christmas every day.

The dangers are obvious: change the pattern of your training to suit your new freedom; over-train because of boredom, and because the facilities are so readily available; eat a ridiculous amount just because it's there; get your bodily timetable out of its normal routine at the crucial stage in its build-up to competition, and wreak havoc with a whole season's meticulous preparation in one careless week.

That said, I have always felt reasonably happy in these surroundings. I've only had one experience of a village seriously below standard—that was Prague, for the 1978 European championships. Dave Moorcroft and I shared a tiny, cold room for a week-and-a-half, and if Dave and I hadn't got on well together it would have been total misery.

The two Olympic villages I've lived in could not have been more contrasting. Moscow was strictly enclosed and fifteen miles out of the city; apart from the times when I was training or racing I think I only left the village compound once in two-and-a-half weeks. I suppose, in retrospect, that it was a bit claustrophobic; a village really should be somewhere you can escape to, not somewhere you feel you want to escape from.

Los Angeles was ideal for me. It was in a residential area, and we could get away for an hour or two whenever we felt like it, just to explore or to look at the shops. The rest of the time I found it relaxing just to meet people, for a change, who weren't involved in running as fast as possible. I remember watching boxers in training and hockey teams at practice, and chatting to lots of neighbours in our part of the village. In Los Angeles some of the more celebrated athletes opted out of the village altogether; they felt that if they got away from the intensely sporting environment and stayed in close contact with their coaches they could ease some of the pressure, but I very much doubt whether it gave them any real advantage, and I'm sure they missed a lot of the fun.

When it comes down to it, villages are no more than collections of people. If you can put up with the people, and they can put up with you, village life is going to be all right.   **SC**

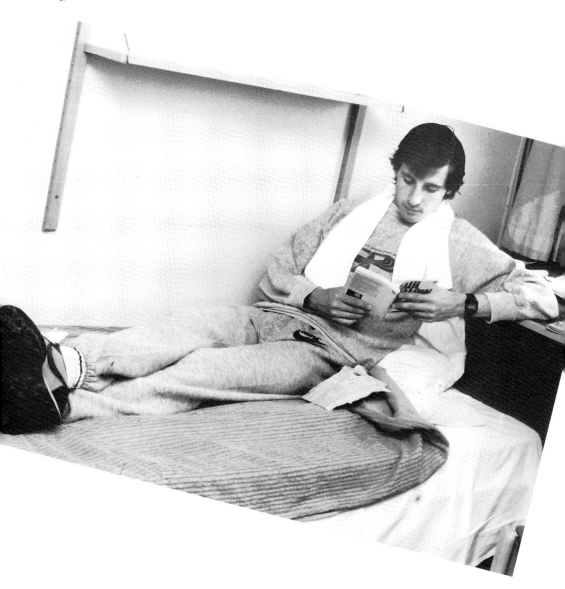

The big day—I

How to prepare for it

The day has arrived, the training is about to be put to the test. So don't let anything fluster you now. As far as equipment is concerned, why not stand by the slogan simple 'Cross-country, road or track, always take your standard pack'. This way you will be ready for almost any emergency.

To run in
1. Vest
2. Shorts
3. Pants (and, for women, running bra)
4. Socks
5. Racing shoes
6. Training shoes

To warm up in
7. Hat
8. Sweatshirt
9. T-shirt
10. Rain top
11. Trousers
12. Rainproof trousers

To change into after run
13. Sweatshirt
14. Trousers
15. Sweater
16. Underpants
17. Shoes
18. Windcheater
19. Socks

Optional extras for running in hot or cold weather
20. Hat
21. T-shirt
22. Training trousers
23. Sweatband
24. Wristbands
25. Gloves

Miscellaneous
26. First aid kit
27. Race acceptance
28. Race details and travel information
29. Pen
30. Map
31. Number (if issued)
32. Safety pins
33. Comb
34. Towel
35. Hold-all

It is also worth taking a large, easily folded plastic refuse bag into which all your gear can be put to keep it dry in bad weather—even on the track the last thing you take off is your tracksuit. The bag can be left with a friend or someone travelling with the team; not every changing-room is a safe place to leave gear.

Experienced runners will know how easy or difficult it is to get food or drink at the various venues. If in doubt, take with you what you know you will need and like—this applies equally if you have a long road or rail journey.

Remember—every race needs preparation; get to the start in the right frame of mind, and half the battle is over. **PC**

Is this a record?

Like putting in golf, or goalkeeping in football, breaking athletic records is very much a sport within a sport, and whenever people start talking about records I always think of Zurich. It is the one place I have been to regularly where the main purpose is to run faster than I have ever run before—and not just because I have greater confidence in Swiss timing!

I have been there every year since 1979, I've broken the 1500 metres and mile world records there, and it has become a place where I always aim to do something special. The closer the public is to the competitors, the greater the intimacy, and this crowd involvement can lift any competitor in a record attempt, whether he is trying to beat the world or whether he is trying to knock a few hundredths off his own personal best, and the mounting clamour and tumult lasts right to the end of the race. In Oslo the fans are closest of all to the action, and in Brussels the crowds are by far the largest; Zurich, though, has the noisiest and perhaps the most intense atmosphere. The Weltklasse meeting is one of the city's major annual events, and as it approaches the newspapers are full of advertisements for tickets and appeals from fans prepared to pay well over face value for a seat. Amongst all this frenzy I am lucky enough to be able to stay with friends just out of town, so I can avoid much of the pre-event tension that many of the athletes are suffering in the hotel in the city centre.

In most cases I prefer to stay with my fellow-competitors, but in Zurich the atmosphere is altogether too highly charged, and I am much happier with the calm of the countryside. My only consideration on the day of the race is to attune myself mentally and physically for the few minutes of effort ahead. I want the fewest possible distractions. In the morning, the second my eyes are open I know it is race day. I get the same familiar feeling of anticipation in my stomach, and I cannot escape from the knowledge that tonight is the night. As soon as I am up I do some light stretching exercises followed by a loosening run through the woods, and I start building myself up for the evening. I feel conscious all the time that I must use as little energy as possible, even to the extent of asking myself whether or not it is worth climbing the stairs to fetch something. It might sound extreme, but if it is not essential I will stay put.

Soon after midday I travel into the city, and book a hotel room for the night. My race is likely to start at around 9.30 in the evening, so I eat a little easily digestible food early in the afternoon, and drink quite a lot of water (a cup of tea is welcome, too, but in Switzerland you can't always count on it). Then it is time for a short nap. I will get up a couple of hours before the race, and take my time putting on my running gear.

Seb storms home ahead of Mike Boit to set a new World Record time for the mile of 3 minutes 48.58 seconds. Zurich, 19 August 1981.

The stadium in Zurich is only a short distance from the hotel, and with the crowd already inside I can walk quietly through the semi-deserted streets listening to the roars of the crowd. With three-quarters of an hour still left I arrive at the warm-up area to begin my final preparations.

Even in a record-breaking attempt, when I am relying on a pre-set plan if everything is going to succeed, the main aim will always be to win—nobody ever set a world record coming second. As soon as the race is over, long before I've had time to glance at a clock, I know from the crowd's reaction whether or not it's been a success—high spirits for a record, relative silence if not. That rather sums up the whole business of tilting at records—it either has been a great night or it hasn't; there are no grey areas.

SC

The big day—II

How to enjoy it

Enjoyment means different things to different people. A family of fun-runners can spend a Sunday afternoon testing their brand new running skills at the back of a fun-run field and go home with a happy, shared sense of something achieved, resolved to get back into their running shoes the following evening with a determination to improve.

In the more rarefied world of competitive athletics, enjoyment comes less easily. The best way—for some the only way—to enjoy the big day is to win. Nothing, absolutely nothing, pleases like success. And if you can't win, a close runner-up in the enjoyment stakes is provided by achieving a personal best.

But for the athlete with a task ahead of him, enjoying the day in the carefree sense is really not on. If you are completely relaxed and free from care it may all feel tremendous fun, but the chances are that you are *too* laid back, and all too likely to turn in a performance lacking concentration and the necessary flow of adrenalin.

Conversely, being too uptight is tiring, and worry is not the best bedfellow for clear-headedness, decision-making and concentration.

Experience should bring you to the ideal balance of tension and aggression to give all your training and planning a chance of success. If it does not, then concentrate on mental control—it can be acquired and developed. It is better to have to work on controlling 'down' than trying to work up the required tension and aggression. Controlling the desire to win is a better base from which to start than having to generate it.

All one can really say about enjoying that big day is that you should do all you can to eliminate unnecessary hassle. Plan your travel arrangements well in advance. Always arrive in good time to pick up your number and your instructions (if you haven't had them through the post), to have a rest and a stretch after the journey, and to have an unhurried and complete warm-up. Always stick to your regular routine—this is psychologically sound and reassuring.

If the presence of friends or other competitors is what you like, that is fine. If, however, you prefer to be quiet and on your own, then before you do anything else seek out somewhere you can rest. This is the time to compose yourself, because other considerations will have to take over once you start your warm-up.

Should your big day be at a track meeting, or a fun-run day with a succession of events, then luck can play a part in your enjoyment. If your event is one of the early ones you can change your gear or put on your tracksuit, then sit back and enjoy the rest of the day.

If your run is scheduled for later, and you have come early with a group, find somewhere comfortable to sit and take the opportunity to watch something different, like the field events,to take your mind off your own race.

One thing is for sure about race days: while they may not give you an actual rest day, they are a lot easier than the average training day. So take comfort from that.   **PC**

June/July

	COURSE	DISTANCE	TIME hour	min	sec

Monday 29

SLEEP _____

HEART _____

WEIGHT _____

AM

PM

Tuesday 30

SLEEP _____

HEART _____

WEIGHT _____

AM

PM

Wednesday 1

SLEEP _____

HEART _____

WEIGHT _____

AM

PM

Thursday 2

SLEEP _____

HEART _____

WEIGHT _____

AM

PM

Friday 3

SLEEP _____

HEART _____

WEIGHT _____

AM

PM

Saturday 4

SLEEP _____

HEART _____

WEIGHT _____

AM

PM

Sunday 5

SLEEP _____

HEART _____

WEIGHT _____

AM

PM

WEEK'S TOTAL DISTANCE

1987

DESCRIPTION	PERCEIVED EFFORT	OBSERVATIONS/INJURIES

AM

PM

AM

PM

AM

PM

AM

PM

AM

PM

AM

PM

AM

PM

GENERAL ASSESSMENT

July

	COURSE	DISTANCE	TIME hour	min	sec

Monday 6
SLEEP

HEART

WEIGHT

AM

PM

Tuesday 7
SLEEP

HEART

WEIGHT

AM

PM

Wednesday 8
SLEEP

HEART

WEIGHT

AM

PM

Thursday 9
SLEEP

HEART

WEIGHT

AM

PM

Friday 10
SLEEP

HEART

WEIGHT

AM

PM

Saturday 11
SLEEP

HEART

WEIGHT

AM

PM

Sunday 12
SLEEP

HEART

WEIGHT

AM

PM

WEEK'S TOTAL DISTANCE

1987

DESCRIPTION

PERCEIVED
EFFORT   OBSERVATIONS/INJURIES

AM

PM

AM

PM

AM

PM

AM

PM

AM

PM

AM

PM

AM

PM

GENERAL ASSESSMENT

July

	COURSE	DISTANCE	TIME hour	min	sec

Monday 13
SLEEP _____
HEART _____
WEIGHT _____

AM

PM

Tuesday 14
SLEEP _____
HEART _____
WEIGHT _____

AM

PM

Wednesday 15
SLEEP _____
HEART _____
WEIGHT _____

AM

PM

Thursday 16
SLEEP _____
HEART _____
WEIGHT _____

AM

PM

Friday 17
SLEEP _____
HEART _____
WEIGHT _____

AM

PM

Saturday 18
SLEEP _____
HEART _____
WEIGHT _____

AM

PM

Sunday 19
SLEEP _____
HEART _____
WEIGHT _____

AM

PM

WEEK'S TOTAL DISTANCE _____

DESCRIPTION	PERCEIVED EFFORT	OBSERVATIONS/INJURIES

AM

_____

PM

AM

_____

PM

AM

_____

PM

AM

_____

PM

AM

_____

PM

AM

_____

PM

AM

_____

PM

GENERAL ASSESSMENT

July

	COURSE	DISTANCE	TIME hour	min	sec

Monday 20
SLEEP

HEART

WEIGHT

AM

PM

Tuesday 21
SLEEP

HEART

WEIGHT

AM

PM

Wednesday 22
SLEEP

HEART

WEIGHT

AM

PM

Thursday 23
SLEEP

HEART

WEIGHT

AM

PM

Friday 24
SLEEP

HEART

WEIGHT

AM

PM

Saturday 25
SLEEP

HEART

WEIGHT

AM

PM

Sunday 26
SLEEP

HEART

WEIGHT

AM

PM

WEEK'S TOTAL DISTANCE

DESCRIPTION	PERCEIVED EFFORT	OBSERVATIONS/INJURIES
AM		
PM		
AM		
PM		
AM		
PM		
AM		
PM		
AM		
PM		
AM		
PM		
AM		
PM		

GENERAL ASSESSMENT

July/August

	COURSE	DISTANCE	TIME hour	min	sec

Monday 27
SLEEP _____

AM

HEART _____

WEIGHT _____

PM

Tuesday 28
SLEEP _____

AM

HEART _____

WEIGHT _____

PM

Wednesday 29
SLEEP _____

AM

HEART _____

WEIGHT _____

PM

Thursday 30
SLEEP _____

AM

HEART _____

WEIGHT _____

PM

Friday 31
SLEEP _____

AM

HEART _____

WEIGHT _____

PM

Saturday 1
SLEEP _____

AM

HEART _____

WEIGHT _____

PM

Sunday 2
SLEEP _____

AM

HEART _____

WEIGHT _____

PM

WEEK'S TOTAL DISTANCE _____

1987

DESCRIPTION

PERCEIVED
EFFORT   OBSERVATIONS/INJURIES

AM

PM

AM

PM

AM

PM

AM

PM

AM

PM

AM

PM

AM

PM

GENERAL ASSESSMENT

August

	COURSE	DISTANCE	TIME hour	min	sec

Monday 3
SLEEP

HEART

WEIGHT

AM

PM

Tuesday 4
SLEEP

HEART

WEIGHT

AM

PM

Wednesday 5
SLEEP

HEART

WEIGHT

AM

PM

Thursday 6
SLEEP

HEART

WEIGHT

AM

PM

Friday 7
SLEEP

HEART

WEIGHT

AM

PM

Saturday 8
SLEEP

HEART

WEIGHT

AM

PM

Sunday 9
SLEEP

HEART

WEIGHT

AM

PM

WEEK'S TOTAL DISTANCE

DESCRIPTION	PERCEIVED EFFORT	OBSERVATIONS/INJURIES
AM		
PM		
AM		
PM		
AM		
PM		
AM		
PM		
AM		
PM		
AM		
PM		
AM		
PM		

GENERAL ASSESSMENT

August

	COURSE	DISTANCE	TIME hour	min	sec

Monday 10

SLEEP

HEART

WEIGHT

AM

PM

Tuesday 11

SLEEP

HEART

WEIGHT

AM

PM

Wednesday 12

SLEEP

HEART

WEIGHT

AM

PM

Thursday 13

SLEEP

HEART

WEIGHT

AM

PM

Friday 14

SLEEP

HEART

WEIGHT

AM

PM

Saturday 15

SLEEP

HEART

WEIGHT

AM

PM

Sunday 16

SLEEP

HEART

WEIGHT

AM

PM

WEEK'S TOTAL DISTANCE

1987

DESCRIPTION

PERCEIVED

PERCEIVED
EFFORT   OBSERVATIONS/INJURIES

AM

PM

AM

PM

AM

PM

AM

PM

AM

PM

AM

PM

AM

PM

GENERAL ASSESSMENT

August

	COURSE	DISTANCE	TIME hour	min	sec

Monday 17
SLEEP _____

HEART _____

WEIGHT _____

AM

PM

Tuesday 18
SLEEP _____

HEART _____

WEIGHT _____

AM

PM

Wednesday 19
SLEEP _____

HEART _____

WEIGHT _____

AM

PM

Thursday 20
SLEEP _____

HEART _____

WEIGHT _____

AM

PM

Friday 21
SLEEP _____

HEART _____

WEIGHT _____

AM

PM

Saturday 22
SLEEP _____

HEART _____

WEIGHT _____

AM

PM

Sunday 23
SLEEP _____

HEART _____

WEIGHT _____

AM

PM

WEEK'S TOTAL DISTANCE

1987

DESCRIPTION	PERCEIVED EFFORT	OBSERVATIONS/INJURIES

AM

PM

AM

PM

AM

PM

AM

PM

AM

PM

AM

PM

AM

PM

GENERAL ASSESSMENT

August

	COURSE		DISTANCE	TIME hour	min	sec

Monday 24
SLEEP _____

HEART _____

WEIGHT _____

AM

PM

Tuesday 25
SLEEP _____

HEART _____

WEIGHT _____

AM

PM

Wednesday 26
SLEEP _____

HEART _____

WEIGHT _____

AM

PM

Thursday 27
SLEEP _____

HEART _____

WEIGHT _____

AM

PM

Friday 28
SLEEP _____

HEART _____

WEIGHT _____

AM

PM

Saturday 29
SLEEP _____

HEART _____

WEIGHT _____

AM

PM

Sunday 30
SLEEP _____

HEART _____

WEIGHT _____

AM

PM

WEEK'S TOTAL DISTANCE _____

DESCRIPTION	PERCEIVED EFFORT	OBSERVATIONS/INJURIES
AM		
PM		
AM		
PM		
AM		
PM		
AM		
PM		
AM		
PM		
AM		
PM		
AM		
PM		

GENERAL ASSESSMENT

August/September

	COURSE	DISTANCE	TIME hour	min	sec

Monday 31
SLEEP

HEART

WEIGHT

AM

PM

Tuesday 1
SLEEP

HEART

WEIGHT

AM

PM

Wednesday 2
SLEEP

HEART

WEIGHT

AM

PM

Thursday 3
SLEEP

HEART

WEIGHT

AM

PM

Friday 4
SLEEP

HEART

WEIGHT

AM

PM

Saturday 5
SLEEP

HEART

WEIGHT

AM

PM

Sunday 6
SLEEP

HEART

WEIGHT

AM

PM

WEEK'S TOTAL DISTANCE

1987

DESCRIPTION	PERCEIVED EFFORT	OBSERVATIONS/INJURIES
AM		
PM		
AM		
PM		
AM		
PM		
AM		
PM		
AM		
PM		
AM		
PM		
AM		
PM		

GENERAL ASSESSMENT

September

	COURSE	DISTANCE	TIME hour	min	sec

Monday 7
SLEEP
HEART
WEIGHT

AM

PM

Tuesday 8
SLEEP
HEART
WEIGHT

AM

PM

Wednesday 9
SLEEP
HEART
WEIGHT

AM

PM

Thursday 10
SLEEP
HEART
WEIGHT

AM

PM

Friday 11
SLEEP
HEART
WEIGHT

AM

PM

Saturday 12
SLEEP
HEART
WEIGHT

AM

PM

Sunday 13
SLEEP
HEART
WEIGHT

AM

PM

WEEK'S TOTAL DISTANCE

DESCRIPTION	PERCEIVED EFFORT	OBSERVATIONS/INJURIES
AM		
PM		
AM		
PM		
AM		
PM		
AM		
PM		
AM		
PM		
AM		
PM		
AM		
PM		

GENERAL ASSESSMENT

September

	COURSE	DISTANCE	TIME hour	min	sec

Monday 14
SLEEP

HEART

WEIGHT

AM

PM

Tuesday 15
SLEEP

HEART

WEIGHT

AM

PM

Wednesday 16
SLEEP

HEART

WEIGHT

AM

PM

Thursday 17
SLEEP

HEART

WEIGHT

AM

PM

Friday 18
SLEEP

HEART

WEIGHT

AM

PM

Saturday 19
SLEEP

HEART

WEIGHT

AM

PM

Sunday 20
SLEEP

HEART

WEIGHT

AM

PM

WEEK'S TOTAL DISTANCE

1987

DESCRIPTION	PERCEIVED EFFORT	OBSERVATIONS/INJURIES

AM

PM

AM

PM

AM

PM

AM

PM

AM

PM

AM

PM

AM

PM

GENERAL ASSESSMENT

September

	COURSE	DISTANCE	TIME hour	min	sec

Monday 21
SLEEP

HEART

WEIGHT

AM

PM

Tuesday 22
SLEEP

HEART

WEIGHT

AM

PM

Wednesday 23
SLEEP

HEART

WEIGHT

AM

PM

Thursday 24
SLEEP

HEART

WEIGHT

AM

PM

Friday 25
SLEEP

HEART

WEIGHT

AM

PM

Saturday 26
SLEEP

HEART

WEIGHT

AM

PM

Sunday 27
SLEEP

HEART

WEIGHT

AM

PM

WEEK'S TOTAL DISTANCE

DESCRIPTION

PERCEIVED
EFFORT   OBSERVATIONS·INJURIES

AM

_____   _____

PM

AM

_____   _____

PM

AM

_____   _____

PM

AM

_____   _____

PM

AM

_____   _____

PM

AM

_____   _____

PM

AM

_____   _____

PM

GENERAL ASSESSMENT

When in Rome

For those of us who had broken through into competitive athletics before the end of the Seventies, these mass marathons and huge fun-run fields came as a bit of a shock. Our idea of a big race field was perhaps a hundred or more at an important regional cross-country championship, or fifty or so pounding along together in a wintry road race.

My first experience of the running boom at first hand was something of a surprise all round. It all began a few hours after I had won the 800 metres at the World Cup in Rome, back in 1981. A few of us were unwinding over a late-night meal, feeling fairly pleased with ourselves and relieved to be out of the blazing Rome sun—I remember Brendan Foster was at the same table, and the commentator Alan Parry. Towards the end of the meal, which had gone on for some time, the conversation culminated in Alan and Brendan challenging each other to run the Rome city half-marathon, scheduled to start in about nine hours' time. I began wondering about the amount of Frascati that had been downed that evening when I heard myself joining in the challenge and saying that I'd come along too.

We weren't a pretty sight the next morning. We struggled along from the hotel to St Peter's Square, all agreeing that the prospect of running rather more than thirteen miles seemed a lot less attractive than it had done the night before, to be confronted with the biggest crowd of runners I had seen on a starting line in my whole career. Brendan had been part of several of these mass runs, but for me it was something quite new—all the more so because, as we had come along on spec, there was no question of our getting VIP treatment up at the front; we piled in as best we could, deep in the throng of ten thousand or more excited Italians waiting for the first nine o'clock chime of St Peter's to set us on our way.

I have never in my life felt such a feeling of claustrophobia. For the first few miles it was like running in a bad dream, like running through treacle. Even though it wasn't meant to be a competitive race, I still had this dreadful feeling of being trapped deep in the pack, unable to get to the leaders who were no doubt racing away from us at the front. Even after quarter of an hour or so, when the sensation of running with so many people became positively pleasant, the competitor in me couldn't shake off the frustration of not being able to get up to the front.

It was a beautiful, historic course, past all the great landmarks of Rome, but it really wasn't until the last few miles that I could begin to appreciate them, or feel anything but part of the mass. By then there was a bit of freedom, a bit of clear road, and a bit of partisan encouragement from a few of the athletes and officials from the British

team who recognised the sweat-stained figure working his way up through the field.

When the dust had died down I found that I'd done a respectable time and finished reasonably well up the field, but if there weren't a number of photographs to prove it I'd be tempted to believe that I'd dreamt the whole thing—from the late-night challenge to the finish line.

Someone said that ours was the first half-marathon run on a Frascati-loading diet! I don't recommend it. **SC**

The importance of strength

A question often asked is 'Why is strength training necessary for runners, particularly for distance runners?' As often as not the questioner is confusing 'maximum strength', the sort that competitive weightlifters strive for, with endurance strength, which every middle distance and long distance runner needs. It is easy enough to understand why sprinters and field events men and women may need strength training, less so why 10,000 metres runners need it. But in fact every athlete needs good all-round strength: have you never seen distance and cross-country runners drop their arms though sheer fatigue, and with it lose any semblance of style? Maintaining good form is essential to successful competition, and you cannot run uphill quickly and repeatedly without strength as well as stamina. The great Ron Clarke, who held so many distance records, said that no athlete could be too strong around the middle.

Assuming you have no previous experience of this type of training, we would suggest the ultra-safe approach—first get yourself strong enough to handle weights without risk. When Seb first embarked on a serious programme of regular sessions with free weights as part of his training, we first found it necessary for him to develop a stronger lower back by means of exercises. Good circuit training, too, will of itself produce good all-round endurance strength, and in addition promote and maintain better flexibility. The best results are obtained by combining both circuits and weights in the programme.

Circuit training   This means a series of exercises done in a set or sets of repetitions considered as one complete cycle. With increasing proficiency the interval between sets can be reduced and the number of cycles increased. As with interval training, the three variables are intensity, frequency and duration.

Ideally circuits are done in a gymnasium where the stations (a different exercise at each) are so spaced around the hall that at the finish of the last exercise you have performed a full circuit and returned to the start.

If you cannot get access to a gym, never mind; you can devise a circuit round the house. Your sit-ups can be done with your toes tucked under the sofa, your chin-ups in a doorway, your bounding up the stairs, your press-ups on any floor (deep press-ups on the arms of a low armchair), weights and 'heavy hand' exercises anywhere.

Weight training   Only running is specific to running, but some exercises can be very close—using weighted wristbands or light dumb-bells and swinging the arms with a running action, for example. If you practise this for at least the duration of the event (and say twice the time for shorter runs like 1,500 metres and 5,000 metres) you will not be one of those who drop their arms during the race.

There are four golden rules for runners using weights:

NEVER lift so as to put unnecessary stress on your lower back (do bench presses rather than heavy overhead lifts).

NEVER repeat maximum lifting within 72 hours; tissue must have time for full recovery.

ALWAYS use a proper lifter's belt.

ALWAYS wear sturdy shoes which are supporting and which have firm heels. Proper lifting shoes are best.

Weight training is best done supervised, certainly when commencing as a beginner. Progress should be steady and careful, and the number of lifts in a set and the number of sets should be increased slowly. As in all training, the programme should be tailored to the individual. The following exercises are all useful:

Circuits
Abdomen Sit-ups (bent knee), leg-raises (hanging or on the floor).
Back Chest raises (on the floor or on a bench).
Trunk Twisting sit-ups (with or without a light weight behind the head), and leg raises.
Legs Step-ups, lunges, hopping, bounding, heel-raising with weights, leg-extensions with weighted feet or ankles.
Ankles Skipping, hopping, wobbleboard.
Arms Push-ups with heels raised (with and without clapping), speedball, punch bag.
All round (shoulders, arms, abdomen, legs) Climbing ropes.
Legs and Ankles Bounding and depth-jumping.

Weights
Pull-overs (for thorax). Flat on floor, arms straightened behind the head holding the weight. Raise the weight above and over the head to touch your body, and return.
Squats (for legs—quads). These can be full or half-squats, though full squats always represent a risk to knees and low back. Half-squats need great care in maintaining balance, and some prefer to do this exercise from a sitting position off a chair or a high bench.
Squats, split and bouncing
Step-ups
Straddle-lifts

All these exercises are best done in repetitions and sets. While they are primarily designed to increase the maximum strength of the various muscles and muscle groups, the endurance content is also important. **PC**

Depth Jumping. To develop elastic strength—the strength involving contractile and stretch components in movements done at speed and under load. A useful exercise for developing sprinting speed and fast uphill running. To avoid injury, keep both feet together at all stages. Pause slightly at the top of each box, the first of which should be slightly lower than the others in the sequence.

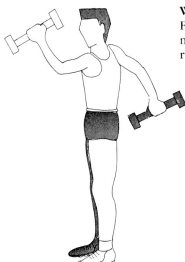

Weights for runners
For developing pure strength, use maximum or near-maximum loads; for strength endurance, practise repetitions with lighter loads.

Arm action
Valuable for sprinters and hill runners, the exercise also helps to prevent arm fatigue. Use weighted grips or light dumb-bells. Simulate, or even slightly exaggerate, the running arm action.

Thighs
The benefit is to the quadriceps of the leading leg, so alternate the leading leg each time. With some experience, and with a lighter load, the exercise can be done dynamically by 'bouncing' from one leading leg to the other.

Thighs and buttocks
The half squat is shown here, with knees only partly bent. Full squats should be attempted only with the greatest care, since they put heavy stress on the fully bent knee.

Thighs and buttocks
Step-ups, from ground to bench. Lead with alternate leg each time.

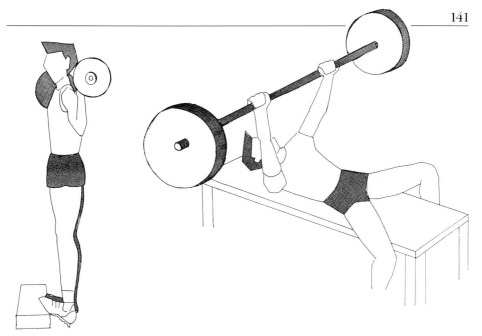

Calf muscles
Heel-raises, lifting the body on the ball of the foot supported by a block of wood. The exercise stretches, as well as strenghthens, the calves.

Triceps and pectorals
(back of the arms and chest)—the famous bench press.

Rib-cage
The bent-arm pull-over, lifting the weight from floor to chest and back, keeping the arms bent at the elbows.

Upper arms (biceps)
'Curling': hold the weight with arms fully extended downwards then, keeping the elbows to your sides, flex the arms until they are fully bent and the weight is under your chin. Keep the body upright.

The pleasures of not running

Once a year I stop running. Literally, after the last race of the season, probably without any sort of wind-down at all, I simply force myself not to place one foot in front of the other at anything above walking pace. I always take at least four full weeks' rest—even longer if it has been a hard season like 1984. I tell myself that all the hard work that I've hammered out of my system has got to have a chance to get back.

I nearly always take a holiday abroad, sometimes lazing on a beach, sometimes walking in Switzerland. For the first few days the feeling is marvellous; I call it the 'lovely-not-to-be-out-running' phase, and after a busy summer on the track I feel I've earned it. At the end of those first few days the feeling changes slightly to one of uncaring contentment—the temptations seem to be winning, and I'm not in the least bothered. I begin to enjoy taking a few liberties, staying out late, eating more than I need to, not caring what time I get up in the morning.

Then, quite suddenly, the rest and the relaxation seem to complete their journey through the system, and I start telling myself that this isn't my kind of lifestyle at all . . . and I find myself turning out cupboards looking for shorts and vest and a pair of running shoes.

It's a strange feeling every year, getting back on the road again. I wouldn't say that I was starting off in autumn at the same level as someone who has never run before, but in relative terms it's not far different from that—a mixture of feeling cumbersome and rather odd. The shoes feel a bit strange on the feet, and I might have a little trouble with my breathing, and I realise with some misgiving that all that lovely fitness has been slowly oozing out of me and that I have got five or six months' hard work ahead of me if I'm going to get back to any satisfactory level of performance by the beginning of the next track season.

It only takes a couple of days to get back in the groove again, and from then on, if I'm lucky, it's all improvement and progress. So why bother?—why take nearly a whole year to work up to a plateau of maximum fitness and ability, and then jump off it every October and let it crumble away?

All I know is that it's absolutely crucial to my being able to continue running year after year. Doctors would probably say it's rubbish, but it feels to me as though I'm somehow replenishing my bodily supplies. It gives a chance for everything to heal up, to take the pressure and strains off the joints. It's a question of letting the body return to some semblance of normality before I start drawing from the well again.

And believe me, after a long, hard season it's absolute bliss.   **SC**

Farther and faster

You're enjoying your running and your occasional venture into a fun run. How about looking ahead a month or two, and planning some real competition on the road, or across country? To do this you are going to have to run farther in training, but above all you are going to want to run faster.

Farther is easy. You learn to run farther simply by running longer distances until you are always able to put together long weekend training runs of 12 to 14 miles in reasonable comfort. A simple build-up distance, combined with adequate rest for full recovery, will do the trick nicely.

The faster bit is not so easy. It is true that the easier the distance running becomes the faster you will be able to run the distance sessions, but this is not training for competition in, say, 10,000-metre road or track races. At the top these days there are no slow runners, not with 53- and 54-second final laps in 5k and 10k races. More and more cross-country and road races, too, are being won with sprint finishes.

'Racing is about speed, so never get too far away from it.' In other words, for most of the year your training should contain the correct balance of speed-preserving or speed-improving elements. Correct training schedules are personal, so we cannot prescribe in detail for everyone, but we can recommend from our own experience the following approach.

At the end of your season, take at least two weeks' rest, even a whole month, from running. This is not complete idleness—there are plenty of other recreational activities, indoors and out, to choose from, and any mix of them will preserve your general level of fitness. But what you are seeking in this rest period is a complete break from the physical repetition of running, to allow the body to complete its repairs and the mind to freshen up in time to return to the fray.

In the next five months you develop and maintain a solid base of distance running. The first eight weeks of this is spent building up to 70 to 80 miles per week, and this is maintained over the following twelve to thirteen weeks.

Not all this mileage is just plain running along. To achieve this 70 to 80 miles profitably will necessitate training twice daily on some days to establish your aerobic fitness. When you are averaging 12 to 14 miles per day, the shorter runs on double days can be run with varying pace as fartlek, and they should include hill-running sessions with both short and steep repetitions, and longer, easier hills of 400 metres to 1,000 metres. This fartlek is a good preparation for the interval training to come. (Never, by the way, make sudden and drastic changes in training. Always make a smooth transition from one stage to the next.)

The interval work provides a powerful stimulus to the stroke/volume of the heart, and it also accustoms the muscles to much faster work without a heavy lactate build-up.

You are now ready for a reduction in mileage and development of your speed endurance. Sustained speed is at the heart of all racing, and it hurts. To master this is absolutely necessary for any racer, and the hard sessions of 600, 800, 1200 and 1600 metre repetitions with short recoveries, which will enable you to produce sustained speed, should be part of the general training for the next two months.

Now you are into your competitive season, and you are using a few selected races to hone your performances to a peak. A useful rule to guide you during this time is that it takes something like 80 per cent of maximum to provide an improving stimulus, but only a 60 per cent loading to maintain that level. Also, long steady running recruits some of the fast twitch (speed) muscle fibres to a more oxidative role (for endurance) which may account for a fall-off in maximum speed. Short sessions of 30 metre and 60 metre accelerations throughout the year will prevent this.

The main enemy of middle- and long-distance runners is injury from over-use. Here the golden rule is: if in doubt, *don't*. You will not suffer dramatic loss of form from a week's lay-off, and there are far too many instances of good performances following short enforced lay-offs for anyone to doubt the wisdom of taking immediate care of injuries.

Most of the year you should take one day off a week, and never less than one day off in every fortnight.

Finally, don't be tempted to race too often. Apart from losing training time, you will tend mentally to devalue each event. It sharpens the mind, and increases the resolve, if you have only a few big moments to work for. **PC**

The hills

Hills make you pant, hills hurt the backs of your legs, and the prospect of tackling hills in a long race—on the road or across country—is enough to discourage all sorts of runners from leaving the comfort of the track. But for most British middle-distance runners, the hills around the country have provided the very basis of their success.

Hills have been part of my day-to-day routine ever since running became serious. I spent nearly all my youth in Sheffield, which is arguably the hilliest city in the country. For me, as a young runner, it was not a question of going out to look for hills to train on, it was more a case of plodding the hills looking for somewhere flat! To get from home to any reasonable stretch of flat road I had to run about two miles uphill in virtually any direction from the front door—so that setting out for a normal distance training run meant the prospect of at least a third, sometimes even two-thirds, of the route on steep hills.

I have always been lucky in one respect: my weight/strength ratio is very high, so when I am faced with a hill, I know that I am not going to have to carry as much weight up it as other runners who may be as strong as me on the flat. Indeed, I find the background of hill running invaluable when I find myself in a road race on a course that is anything but absolutely level. Most road runners will tackle a hill as economically as possible, conserving energy where they can and leaving their real effort for the flat. It is a good psychological weapon, as well as a tactical one, to have the confidence to attack *on* the hill; even if it doesn't break your opponents' will, or give you a tangible advantage, it will almost certainly help to break their rhythm.

Training on hills sounds painful, but even a hard session doesn't hurt me in the way that it might be expected to. The heart rate goes up, of course, and the breathing becomes a little harder, and I feel the effort in areas where I don't feel it in a normal training session—the hamstrings and the back of the thighs, sometimes, and, if I'm not in top condition, in the shoulders and the upper arms when I'm working hard. But if I *am* labouring, and my stride is shortening drastically, it probably means the hill is too steep, which in turn means that I am not getting the benefit I should be.

I look for reasonably stiff, gradual stretches of 100 yards or 150 yards each—not longer— which allow me to run up them at a natural, fast, rhythmic pace, and give me enough time for recovery as I jog down again to the start. (Note the 'jog down'—not run down. I'm quite happy running uphill, but running downhill is no fun at all: it hammers the joints, the tendency to lean backwards puts a dreadful strain on the lower back, and it turns the knees and ankles into overworked shock-absorbers.)

That apart, I have a great affection for the hills, and I know dozens of other athletes who feel the same. All of us have memories of our early running years, of far too many cross-country races every season, of running for the school in the morning and the local club in the afternoon, up and down the tracks and banks of squelchy, windswept parks with the promise of no more than a communal tin bath in a school playground in which to scrape off the surface mud.

It's hardly glamorous, but it's invaluable grounding for any young runner.   **SC**

The way to a painless marathon

If there ever was a painless marathon, and I doubt it, then it was for the winner alone, and then only for that short exuberant moment of victory.

A marathon is a hard, prolonged effort, and what follows here is no more than a collection of hints and guidelines to soften the effects and ward off distress or lasting injury. The most obvious advice, often given but too often not thoroughly thought through, is to be properly prepared before starting, which means being adequately trained and equipped. This does *not* mean being near-exhausted with excess training mileage (usually to someone else's magic schedule), but trained *and rested*.

In our book *Running for Fitness* we considered a first-timer aiming for a marathon time of four hours (and we repeat that schedule here in the appendix). Now we shall look at a serious runner trying to beat 2 hours 30 minutes—a very different kettle of fish.

At the heart of all distance running is a carefully and assiduously acquired sense of pace judgement, a sense that must never fail you whatever the weather conditions, or however tired you may become.

Look at these few figures:

PACE PER MILE	MARATHON TIME
5 minutes 00 seconds	2 hours 11 minutes 6 seconds
5 minutes 30 seconds	2 hours 24 minutes 12 seconds
5 minutes 42 seconds	2 hours 29 minutes 26 seconds
5 minutes 45 seconds	2 hours 30 minutes 46 seconds

That seemingly insignificant three seconds difference is only fifteen yards, or perhaps eight strides, each mile. But at the end of the marathon it has become the difference between running half a minute under, and running almost one minute over, the target time of two-and-a-half hours. Pace judgement, we repeat, is critical. Although much of your training will be done faster than race pace, you must nevertheless do enough work at your intended racing speed so as not to run too fast too early or to fall behind the clock and leave an impossible task towards the end of your marathon.

It cannot be stated too often that a good training schedule is tailored to the individual, but in order to give training hints some generalising is necessary.

First, it will take a naturally very talented athlete to achieve a two-and-a-half-hour marathon on only 60 miles per week, and we would suggest at least 75 miles per week as the steady base of your training. This basic mileage should be carried out at a fairly brisk pace and, depending upon the distance run in any one session, vary between 5 minutes and 5 minutes 30 seconds per mile.

There should always be one good long run every week, between 15 and 20 miles, and on a couple of occasions you should run the full distance, at less than race pace, to get the measure of the race and as a confidence booster.

These full-distance runs should not be attempted too close together, nor within a month of the big race.

Don't do all your running at even pace, and don't restrict yourself to the road. Your training must include some harder fartlek sessions and plenty of repetitions on long hills, as well as some really hard speed endurance work using 800-metre, 1200-metre

A triumph of training: Steve Jones wins the 1985 London Marathon.

and 1600-metre repetitions. Throughout all your training, regular timed runs over measured distances should be included so that, tired or fresh, you can judge pace with accuracy.

Remember that mile posts will not always be conveniently (or accurately) placed, and concentration, which is so important when running, does not mean trying to memorise every mile time or attempting continuous mental arithmetic.

A crucial part of your training will be taking part in road races over six and ten miles, as well as one or two half-marathons. Here the emphasis will not be on winning, but on getting the feel of sustainable pace amid the distractions of other runners surging or falling back. Except perhaps for the half-marathons, all these races should be treated as training runs, without resting up the day before. A regular once-a-week or once-a-fortnight rest day should be part of your usual routine (don't worry, you *do* have time for a rest day on 75 miles per week—some of your schedule will involve twice-a-day training).

It is also worth remembering that it can take the body four weeks or more to adjust to an increase in stress, so do not hurry the stages of your build-up at any time, and be specially careful after an enforced lay-off.

Drinking   If you have not already done so, you must work out by practice the quantity and frequency of fluid intake that suits you best. The ideal quantity is the most that you can get down without upsetting yourself, since the running body will always be getting rid of fluid faster than your stomach can absorb it, particularly in summer when dehydration is a very real risk.

Eating   Carting around unwanted fat is very energy-expensive, but it is most unlikely that on 75 miles per week you will be having to cut down on your food intake. If you have stepped up your mileage, then it is likely that you have stepped up your eating. But don't merely increase your intake of carbohydrate—keep the meals balanced.

After heavy training it takes as much as two or three days to replenish your depleted glycogen store While you can 'run through' your shorter races, using them as part of the training, you must taper off for a full marathon so that you start with the batteries fully charged.

Prior to the race it is not necessary to go on a 'bleed-out' routine, but a high-carbohydrate diet for three or four days, together with very light training, will give you an increased store of glycogen. By light training we mean as little as five or six miles a day, performed at a lot less than race pace. This will keep you ticking over nicely and will not diminish our glycogen build-up.

Close to the race, eat only foods that are easily digested and leave the stomach quickly—like pasta—and eat nothing in the three hours before the start. Avoid eating meat or fatty food in your pre-race meal. It is claimed that drinking a couple of cups of black, unsweetened coffee one hour before a marathon will assist in the liberation of free fatty acids upon which the long-distance runner calls.

Gear   In marathon running heat dissipation is a governing factor in how well you perform, so the simplest rule for clothing is 'little and light'. This may include reflective and face-shading headgear—the hair and the face present large areas for absorbing the heat of the sun, and anything which limits that is worth considering (remember what it did for Joan Benoit in that Olympic marathon in Los Angeles).

Not all marathons are run in warm weather, though. Rain, wind and low temperatures can make the race thoroughly uncomfortable, particularly for the slower runner. In these conditions it might be as well to consider covering the more static parts of the body (shoulders and upper arms, for example), by wearing a quarter-sleeve singlet under your running vest, or even a long-sleeved vest.

The marathon mileage schedules will be found in the Appendix on page 189.   **PC**

September/October

Monday 28

SLEEP

HEART

WEIGHT

AM

PM

Tuesday 29

SLEEP

HEART

WEIGHT

AM

PM

Wednesday 30

SLEEP

HEART

WEIGHT

AM

PM

Thursday 1

SLEEP

HEART

WEIGHT

AM

PM

Friday 2

SLEEP

HEART

WEIGHT

AM

PM

Saturday 3

SLEEP

HEART

WEIGHT

AM

PM

Sunday 4

SLEEP

HEART

WEIGHT

AM

PM

WEEK'S TOTAL DISTANCE

DESCRIPTION

PERCEIVED
EFFORT   OBSERVATIONS/INJURIES

AM

PM

AM

PM

AM

PM

AM

PM

AM

PM

AM

PM

AM

PM

GENERAL ASSESSMENT

October

	COURSE	DISTANCE	TIME hour	min	sec

Monday 5
SLEEP _____
HEART _____
WEIGHT _____

AM

PM

Tuesday 6
SLEEP _____
HEART _____
WEIGHT _____

AM

PM

Wednesday 7
SLEEP _____
HEART _____
WEIGHT _____

AM

PM

Thursday 8
SLEEP _____
HEART _____
WEIGHT _____

AM

PM

Friday 9
SLEEP _____
HEART _____
WEIGHT _____

AM

PM

Saturday 10
SLEEP _____
HEART _____
WEIGHT _____

AM

PM

Sunday 11
SLEEP _____
HEART _____
WEIGHT _____

AM

PM

WEEK'S TOTAL DISTANCE _____

DESCRIPTION

AM

_____   _____

PM

_____

AM

_____   _____

PM

_____

AM

_____   _____

PM

_____

AM

_____   _____

PM

_____

AM

_____   _____

PM

_____

AM

_____   _____

PM

_____

AM

_____   _____

PM

_____

GENERAL ASSESSMENT

October

	COURSE	DISTANCE	TIME hour	min	sec

Monday 12
SLEEP _____

HEART _____

WEIGHT _____

AM

PM

Tuesday 13
SLEEP _____

HEART _____

WEIGHT _____

AM

PM

Wednesday 14
SLEEP _____

HEART _____

WEIGHT _____

AM

PM

Thursday 15
SLEEP _____

HEART _____

WEIGHT _____

AM

PM

Friday 16
SLEEP _____

HEART _____

WEIGHT _____

AM

PM

Saturday 17
SLEEP _____

HEART _____

WEIGHT _____

AM

PM

Sunday 18
SLEEP _____

HEART _____

WEIGHT _____

AM

PM

WEEK'S TOTAL DISTANCE _____

DESCRIPTION

AM

_____   _____

PM

AM

_____   _____

PM

AM

_____   _____

PM

AM

_____   _____

PM

AM

_____   _____

PM

AM

_____   _____

PM

AM

_____   _____

PM

GENERAL ASSESSMENT

October

	COURSE	DISTANCE	TIME hour	min	sec

Monday 19
SLEEP
HEART
WEIGHT

AM

PM

Tuesday 20
SLEEP
HEART
WEIGHT

AM

PM

Wednesday 21
SLEEP
HEART
WEIGHT

AM

PM

Thursday 22
SLEEP
HEART
WEIGHT

AM

PM

Friday 23
SLEEP
HEART
WEIGHT

AM

PM

Saturday 24
SLEEP
HEART
WEIGHT

AM

PM

Sunday 25
SLEEP
HEART
WEIGHT

AM

PM

WEEK'S TOTAL DISTANCE

DESCRIPTION	PERCEIVED EFFORT	OBSERVATIONS/INJURIES

AM

_____

PM

AM

_____

PM

AM

_____

PM

AM

_____

PM

AM

_____

PM

AM

_____

PM

AM

_____

PM

GENERAL ASSESSMENT

October/November

	COURSE	DISTANCE	TIME hour	min	sec

Monday 26
SLEEP _____

AM

HEART _____

PM

WEIGHT _____

Tuesday 27
SLEEP _____

AM

HEART _____

PM

WEIGHT _____

Wednesday 28
SLEEP _____

AM

HEART _____

PM

WEIGHT _____

Thursday 29
SLEEP _____

AM

HEART _____

PM

WEIGHT _____

Friday 30
SLEEP _____

AM

HEART _____

PM

WEIGHT _____

Saturday 31
SLEEP _____

AM

HEART _____

PM

WEIGHT _____

Sunday 1
SLEEP _____

AM

HEART _____

PM

WEIGHT _____

WEEK'S TOTAL DISTANCE

1987

DESCRIPTION	PERCEIVED EFFORT	OBSERVATIONS/INJURIES

AM

_____ _____

PM

AM

_____ _____

PM

AM

_____ _____

PM

AM

_____ _____

PM

AM

_____ _____

PM

AM

_____ _____

PM

AM

_____ _____

PM

GENERAL ASSESSMENT

November

	COURSE	DISTANCE	TIME hour	min	sec

Monday 2
SLEEP

HEART

WEIGHT

AM

PM

Tuesday 3
SLEEP

HEART

WEIGHT

AM

PM

Wednesday 4
SLEEP

HEART

WEIGHT

AM

PM

Thursday 5
SLEEP

HEART

WEIGHT

AM

PM

Friday 6
SLEEP

HEART

WEIGHT

AM

PM

Saturday 7
SLEEP

HEART

WEIGHT

AM

PM

Sunday 8
SLEEP

HEART

WEIGHT

AM

PM

WEEK'S TOTAL DISTANCE

1987

DESCRIPTION

PERCEIVED
EFFORT   OBSERVATIONS/INJURIES

AM

PM

AM

PM

AM

PM

AM

PM

AM

PM

AM

PM

AM

PM

GENERAL ASSESSMENT

November

	COURSE		DISTANCE	TIME hour	min	sec

Monday 9
SLEEP

HEART

WEIGHT

AM

PM

Tuesday 10
SLEEP

HEART

WEIGHT

AM

PM

Wednesday 11
SLEEP

HEART

WEIGHT

AM

PM

Thursday 12
SLEEP

HEART

WEIGHT

AM

PM

Friday 13
SLEEP

HEART

WEIGHT

AM

PM

Saturday 14
SLEEP

HEART

WEIGHT

AM

PM

Sunday 15
SLEEP

HEART

WEIGHT

AM

PM

WEEK'S TOTAL DISTANCE

DESCRIPTION

AM

_____   _____

PM

AM

_____   _____

PM

AM

_____   _____

PM

AM

_____   _____

PM

AM

_____   _____

PM

AM

_____   _____

PM

AM

_____   _____

PM

GENERAL ASSESSMENT

November

	COURSE	DISTANCE	TIME hour	min	sec

Monday 16
SLEEP _____

HEART _____

WEIGHT _____

AM _____

PM _____

Tuesday 17
SLEEP _____

HEART _____

WEIGHT _____

AM _____

PM _____

Wednesday 18
SLEEP _____

HEART _____

WEIGHT _____

AM _____

PM _____

Thursday 19
SLEEP _____

HEART _____

WEIGHT _____

AM _____

PM _____

Friday 20
SLEEP _____

HEART _____

WEIGHT _____

AM _____

PM _____

Saturday 21
SLEEP _____

HEART _____

WEIGHT _____

AM _____

PM _____

Sunday 22
SLEEP _____

HEART _____

WEIGHT _____

AM _____

PM _____

WEEK'S TOTAL DISTANCE _____

1987

DESCRIPTION

PERCEIVED
EFFORT OBSERVATIONS/INJURIES

AM

PM

AM

PM

AM

PM

AM

PM

AM

PM

AM

PM

AM

PM

GENERAL ASSESSMENT

November

	COURSE	DISTANCE	TIME hour	min	sec

Monday 23
SLEEP
HEART
WEIGHT

AM

PM

Tuesday 24
SLEEP
HEART
WEIGHT

AM

PM

Wednesday 25
SLEEP
HEART
WEIGHT

AM

PM

Thursday 26
SLEEP
HEART
WEIGHT

AM

PM

Friday 27
SLEEP
HEART
WEIGHT

AM

PM

Saturday 28
SLEEP
HEART
WEIGHT

AM

PM

Sunday 29
SLEEP
HEART
WEIGHT

AM

PM

WEEK'S TOTAL DISTANCE

1987

DESCRIPTION	PERCEIVED EFFORT	OBSERVATIONS/INJURIES
AM		
PM		
AM		
PM		
AM		
PM		
AM		
PM		
AM		
PM		
AM		
PM		
AM		
PM		

GENERAL ASSESSMENT

November/December

	COURSE	DISTANCE	TIME hour	min	sec

Monday 30
SLEEP _____

HEART _____

WEIGHT _____

AM

PM

Tuesday 1
SLEEP _____

HEART _____

WEIGHT _____

AM

PM

Wednesday 2
SLEEP _____

HEART _____

WEIGHT _____

AM

PM

Thursday 3
SLEEP _____

HEART _____

WEIGHT _____

AM

PM

Friday 4
SLEEP _____

HEART _____

WEIGHT _____

AM

PM

Saturday 5
SLEEP _____

HEART _____

WEIGHT _____

AM

PM

Sunday 6
SLEEP _____

HEART _____

WEIGHT _____

AM

PM

WEEK'S TOTAL DISTANCE _____

DESCRIPTION	PERCEIVED EFFORT	OBSERVATIONS/INJURIES
AM		
PM		
AM		
PM		
AM		
PM		
AM		
PM		
AM		
PM		
AM		
PM		
AM		
PM		

GENERAL ASSESSMENT

December

	COURSE	DISTANCE	TIME hour	min	sec

Monday 7
SLEEP

HEART

WEIGHT

AM

PM

Tuesday 8
SLEEP

HEART

WEIGHT

AM

PM

Wednesday 9
SLEEP

HEART

WEIGHT

AM

PM

Thursday 10
SLEEP

HEART

WEIGHT

AM

PM

Friday 11
SLEEP

HEART

WEIGHT

AM

PM

Saturday 12
SLEEP

HEART

WEIGHT

AM

PM

Sunday 13
SLEEP

HEART

WEIGHT

AM

PM

WEEK'S TOTAL DISTANCE

DESCRIPTION

AM

PM

AM

PM

AM

PM

AM

PM

AM

PM

AM

PM

AM

PM

GENERAL ASSESSMENT

December

	COURSE	DISTANCE	TIME hour	min	sec

Monday 14
SLEEP

HEART

WEIGHT

AM

PM

Tuesday 15
SLEEP

HEART

WEIGHT

AM

PM

Wednesday 16
SLEEP

HEART

WEIGHT

AM

PM

Thursday 17
SLEEP

HEART

WEIGHT

AM

PM

Friday 18
SLEEP

HEART

WEIGHT

AM

PM

Saturday 19
SLEEP

HEART

WEIGHT

AM

PM

Sunday 20
SLEEP

HEART

WEIGHT

AM

PM

WEEK'S TOTAL DISTANCE

DESCRIPTION	PERCEIVED EFFORT	OBSERVATIONS/INJURIES

AM

_____   _____

PM

AM

_____   _____

PM

AM

_____   _____

PM

AM

_____   _____

PM

AM

_____   _____

PM

AM

_____   _____

PM

AM

_____   _____

PM

GENERAL ASSESSMENT

December

	COURSE	DISTANCE	TIME hour	min	sec

Monday 21
SLEEP _____

HEART _____

WEIGHT _____

AM

PM

Tuesday 22
SLEEP _____

HEART _____

WEIGHT _____

AM

PM

Wednesday 23
SLEEP _____

HEART _____

WEIGHT _____

AM

PM

Thursday 24
SLEEP _____

HEART _____

WEIGHT _____

AM

PM

Friday 25
SLEEP _____

HEART _____

WEIGHT _____

AM

PM

Saturday 26
SLEEP _____

HEART _____

WEIGHT _____

AM

PM

Sunday 27
SLEEP _____

HEART _____

WEIGHT _____

AM

PM

WEEK'S TOTAL DISTANCE

1987

DESCRIPTION	PERCEIVED EFFORT	OBSERVATIONS/INJURIES
AM		
PM		
AM		
PM		
AM		
PM		
AM		
PM		
AM		
PM		
AM		
PM		
AM		
PM		

GENERAL ASSESSMENT

December 1987/January 1988

	COURSE	DISTANCE	TIME hour	min	sec

Monday 28
SLEEP

HEART

WEIGHT

AM

PM

Tuesday 29
SLEEP

HEART

WEIGHT

AM

PM

Wednesday 30
SLEEP

HEART

WEIGHT

AM

PM

Thursday 31
SLEEP

HEART

WEIGHT

AM

PM

Friday 1
SLEEP

HEART

WEIGHT

AM

PM

Saturday 2
SLEEP

HEART

WEIGHT

AM

PM

Sunday 3
SLEEP

HEART

WEIGHT

AM

PM

WEEK'S TOTAL DISTANCE

DESCRIPTION	PERCEIVED EFFORT	OBSERVATIONS/INJURIES

AM

PM

AM

PM

AM

PM

AM

PM

AM

PM

AM

PM

AM

PM

GENERAL ASSESSMENT

Race summary

DATE	EVENT	DISTANCE	PLACE AND TIME	WINNERS NAME AND TIME	REMARKS	see training page

DATE	EVENT	DISTANCE	PLACE AND TIME	WINNERS NAME AND TIME	REMARKS	*see training page*

Annual mileage and training

ACTIVITY	JAN	FEB	MAR	APR	MAY	JUNE	JULY	AUG	SEPT	OCT	NOV	DEC	TOTAL
Circuits hours													
Weights hours													
Steady distance work													
Fast distance work													
Fartlek work													
Speed hours													
Speed endurance													

Race schedules

Race Schedules

Among runners of all standards—runners for fitness, for relaxation, for friendly competition and for glory—there are literally hundreds of specially tailored and widely differing schedules. Here we are providing notes for a few of the more common targets for beginners and recently established runners: an informal three-mile run; one of the 10-kilometre races that are gaining so fast in popularity; a get-round-at-all-costs marathon; and, for those who are keen to go on improving, a year's mileage schedule for a more ambitious marathon time.

1. Three-mile fun run

We shall assume that you have read some of the notes earlier in the Diary on first steps to running and on what to wear, and possibly that you have taken part for fun in an informal event or two. This schedule will enable you to attack a three-mile course with confidence and complete it in a satisfying time.

This schedule is based on a target pace of 7 minutes per mile—a finishing time, therefore, of about 21 minutes. Your training, to assure that you can maintain that pace, is split three ways:

A—Over-distance running for good all-round stamina (say an occasional run of six to eight miles).
B—Running a mile at race-pace or better; recovery for two or three minutes; then running another mile; then another recovery; then the third mile. Gradually cut down the recovery time.
C—Running a mile at race pace, then carry on until you start to slow significantly; extend these sessions until you can carry on for a full *four* miles at your three-mile race pace.

This four-week-plan can be altered to meet your work and family needs, but it is best to stick to a routine whenever you can, and try to have your rest day on the same day each week.

Three-mile fun run schedule

Week 1
Monday
Run 6 miles steady at your comfortable pace
Tuesday
1 mile in 7-mins. Jog home (J.H.) if you are training within a mile or two of your home
Wednesday
Rest
Thursday
1 mile in 7-min. Rest 3-min. Run 1 mile in 7-min.
Friday
6 miles steady (as Monday)
Saturday
1½ miles in 7-min (J.H.)
Sunday
6 miles steady

Week 2
Monday
3 x 1 mile at 7-min pace, with a 3-min rest between each mile (J.H.)
Tuesday
6 miles steady
Wednesday
Rest
Thursday
2 miles in 14-min (J.H.)
Friday
6 miles steady
Saturday
4 x 1 mile at 7-min pace, with a 2-min rest between each mile (J.H.)
Sunday
6 miles steady

Week 3
Monday
2½ miles in 17½-min (J.H.)
Tuesday
6 miles steady
Wednesday
Rest
Thursday
4 x 1 mile at 7-min pace, with 1½-min rest between each mile (J.H.)
Friday
8 miles steady
Saturday
3 miles in 21-min (J.H.)
Sunday
6 miles steady

Week 4
Monday
3½ miles in 24½-min (J.H.)
Tuesday
8 miles steady
Wednesday
Rest
Thursday
4 x 1 mile at 7-min pace, with ½-min rest between each mile (J.H.)
Friday
3 miles easy
Saturday
Rest
Sunday
RACE

10 kilometre race schedule

Week 1	WARM-UP MILES	SESSION	WARM DOWN MILES	TOTAL MILES
Sunday	3	4 x 1,600 metres	3	10
Monday	–	1 hour fartlek	–	8
Tuesday	3	8 x 800 metres	3	10
Wednesday	–	Road run	–	8
Thursday	3	16 x 200 metres	3	8
Friday	–	1 hour fartlek	–	8
Saturday	*	3,000 metre time trial	3	6
			Total	58

Week 2

Sunday	3	4 x 400 metres	3	7
Monday	–	7 miles a.m., 8 miles p.m.	–	15
Tuesday	*	1 x 300m, 2 x 200m, 4 x 100m, 8 x 60m.	3	5
Wednesday	–	Hilly fartlek	–	7
Thursday	3	3 x 2,000 metres	3	10
Friday	–	Rest	–	–
Saturday	*	1,500 metre race	3	5
			Total	49

Week 3

Sunday	–	12 miles	–	12
Monday	–	5 miles a.m., 4 miles p.m.	–	9
Tuesday	3	8 x 800 metres	3	10
Wednesday	–	5 miles a.m., 4 miles p.m.	–	9
Thursday	3	16 x 200 metres	3	8
Friday	–	1 hour fartlek	–	8
Saturday	*	3,000 metre time trial	3	6
			Total	62

Week 4

Sunday	3	4 x 400 metres	3	7
Monday	–	Hilly 8 miles	–	8
Tuesday	*	1 x 300m, 2 x 200m, 4 x 100m, 8 x 60m	3	5
Wednesday	–	1 hour fartlek	–	8
Thursday	2	3 miles (90% effort)	3	8
Friday	–	Rest	–	–
Saturday	*	RACE 10,000 metres	3	9
			Total	47

2. Ten-kilometre (6¼ mile) race

This is a schedule for athletes with proven ability, but it can readily be adapted to the needs of the slower or older runner so long as they all observe the one golden rule: for every session there must be adequate time for recovery. When peaking for an event, 'one hard and two easy' is the safest way of planning the training days.

After four weeks of this schedule you should find that you can maintain the same level of fitness easily with one long run (10–14 miles) per week, shorter runs at a moderate pace and a few speed drills and accelerations.

*All time trials, races and speed sessions must be preceded by a full warm-up, including suppling and stretching—NOT a 3-mile running warm-up.

3. Finish-at-all-costs marathon

Choose your own target time, but if you can maintain the relatively gentle pace of 9 minutes 9 seconds per mile for the full distance, you will finish your marathon in under four hours.

This chart, which builds up in its peak period to around 50 miles per week, should help you prepare for such a marathon. It is based largely on increasingly long runs to increase stamina, and puts little or no emphasis on speed training. It will help your confidence for the big day if one of your long runs about a month before your marathon is a half-marathon race; use it as a training run, and also to get a taste of the atmosphere at a formal, organised race.

Week	Tues	Weds	Thurs	Fri	Sat	Sun	Mon	Total
1	6	5	ss	6	5	8	ss	30
2	5	6·	ss	5	6	10	ss	32
3	6	6	ss	6	6	10	ss	34
4	6	8	ss	8	6	8	ss	36
5	5	8	ss	8	5	12	ss	38
6	10	6	ss	9	7	8	ss	40
7	11	5	ss	9	7	9	ss	41
8	6	7	ss	7	6	16	ss	42
9	6	8	6	8	6	10	ss	44
10	10	7	ss	10	7	12	ss	46
11	6	8	ss	8	6	20	ss	48
12	6	10	8	10	8	8	ss	50
13	12	5	6	6	5	16	ss	50
14	6	10	6	10	6	10	ss	48
15	7	10	ss	7	ss	16	ss	40
16	5	6	ss	6	8	8	ss	33
17	6	jog 5	jog 4	ss	ss	RACE		15
							Training total 667	

(ss=suppleness and stretching on rest day)

4. The quicker marathon

Once you are aiming at 8-minute-per-mile pace or faster, your target time will not be strictly related to your total training mileage, though a runner aiming for two-and-a-half hours will want perhaps 20 miles a week more than the same runner with a target of three-and-a-half hours. The faster the target, the greater the emphasis placed on speed work etc (see our notes on marathon training on page 151). This chart gives a build-up mileage guide over a complete year's training, aimed at a marathon in September.

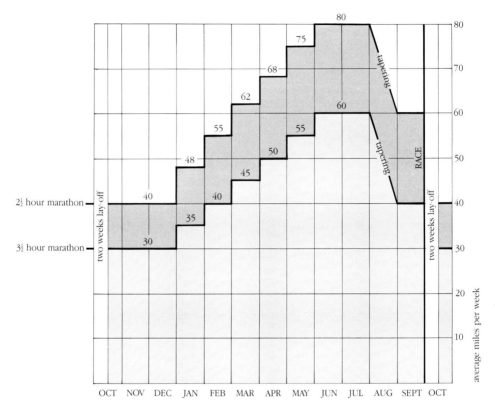

Running in company

Sooner or later you will want to join a club—because you are bored with running alone, because you want some competition, or just because you want to save the extra 50p that non-members of AAA-affiliated clubs have to pay to enter road runs.

Running Clubs For serious runners (not necessarily fast ones) and for aspiring athletes, there are literally hundreds of clubs throughout the country. The Amateur Athletics Association (which has its own membership scheme) has a list of all of them; a letter to your regional AAA office,enclosing a stamped addressed envelope, should get you the information you want:

Southern Counties AAA and England and Wales Women's AAA—Francis House, Francis Street, London SW1 1DL.
Midland AAA—Devonshire House, High Street, Deritend, Birmingham B12 0LP.
Northern Counties AAA—Studio 44, Bluecoat Chambers, Liverpool L1B XC3.
Welsh AAA—54 Charles Street, Cardiff.
Scottish AAA and Scottish Women's AAA—16 Royal Crescent, Glasgow G3 7SL.
Northern Ireland AAA—20 Kernan Park, Portadown, Co. Armagh, Northern Ireland.
Northern Ireland Women's AAA—Tir na Nog, Old Calgorm Road, Ballymena, N. Ireland.

For direct registration to the AAA's own scheme, write to:

AAA Registration Scheme, PO Box 27, Basildon, Essex SS–5 6DW.

Jogging Clubs Beginners, and those without any pretensions to competition at this stage, may prefer the friendly take-it-or-leave-it informality of the local jogging club. These, too, are numerous; some are well established and flourishing, others come and go at the whim of a small membership. Both *Running Magazine* and *Today's Runner* have published lists of established jogging clubs, and up-date their lists from time to time. *Running Magazine*'s main list was in their April 1984 issue, *Today's Runner*'s list in their issue of October 1985.

Cross-Country Clubs For those contemplating a season in the mud, many running clubs organise come-and-try-it cross-country events at the end of the autumn. If you have trouble finding such an event, a letter to any of the following addresses should help:

England	*Men:* Barry Wallman, 7 Wolsey Way, Cherry Hinton, Cambridge.
	Women: Vera Duerdin, 10 Anderton Close, Bury, Lancs.
Scotland	*Men:* Ian Clifton, 38 Silverknowes Drive, Edinburgh 4.
	Women: Mrs J. Ward, 144 Canberra Avenue, Dalmuir West, Clydebank.
Wales	*Men:* G. Collins, Harriers Haunt, 40 Twyniteg, Killey, Swansea.
	Women: Margaret Elgie, 19 Coedbach, Highlight Park, Barry, South Glamorgan.
N. Ireland	*Men:* Northern Ireland Sports Council (Athletics), 2 Upper Malone Road, Belfast 9.
	Women: Pam Reece, 28 Ravelston Avenue, Glengormley, N. Ireland.

Reading about running

With the running boom has come a predictable flurry of reading matter for runners of all standards and all levels of aspiration. Of the selection below, all published in Britain, the long-established *Athletics Weekly* is the serious club runner's handbook, with its up-to-date features on the dominant figures of the sport liberally interspersed with detailed race results. *Running Magazine* and, more recently, *Today's Runner* have aimed at a broader spectrum, with bright and practical training and equipment hints for beginners and fun-runners as well as for their faster counterparts.

Athletics Weekly
World Athletics and Sporting Publications Ltd, 342 High Street, Rochester, Kent ME1 1ED. (*weekly*)

Running Magazine
57–61 Mortimer Street, London W1N 7TD. (*monthly*)

Today's Runner
EMAP Pursuit Publishing Ltd., Bretton Court, Bretton, Peterborough PE3 8DZ. (*monthly*)

Athletics Today
Peterson Publishing Co Ltd, Peterson House, Northbank, Berryhill Industrial Estate, Droitwich, Worcs WR9 9BL. (*monthly*)

Marathon and Distance Runner
Peterson Publishing Co Ltd (as above). (*monthly*)

Running Review
Ron Hill Sports, PO Box 11, Hyde, Cheshire. (*monthly*)